THE MOST

Wonderful

TIME OF THE
YEAR

More books by Ace Collins

Nonfiction
Man's Best Hero
Music for Your Heart

Fiction
The Fruitcake Murders
Hollywood Lost
The Color of Justice
The Cutting Edge
Darkness Before Dawn
The Christmas Star

THE MOST *Wonderful* TIME OF THE YEAR

A COUNTDOWN TO CHRISTMAS

ACE COLLINS

ABINGDON PRESS

NASHVILLE

THE MOST WONDERFUL TIME OF THE YEAR

A COUNTDOWN TO CHRISTMAS

Library of Congress Cataloging-in-Publication Data

Names: Collins, Ace, author.
Title: The most wonderful time of the year : a countdown to Christmas / Ace Collins.
Description: First [edition]. | Nashville, Tennessee : Abingdon Press, 2016.
Identifiers: LCCN 2016021753 | ISBN 9781501822605 (pbk.)
Subjects: LCSH: Christmas—Miscellanea. | Advent—Miscellanea.
Classification: LCC BV45 .C5893 2016 | DDC 242/.33—dc23 LC record available at https://lccn.loc.gov/2016021753

The majority of the ingredients (such as the essential oils) used in the "Pamper / Feed the One You Love!" sections can be found at natural and organic food markets. For storage containers or craft items, visit your local arts and crafts stores.

All song lyrics are in the public domain.

16 17 18 19 20 21 22 23 24—10 9 8 7 6 5 4 3 2 1

MANUFACTURED IN THE UNITED STATES OF AMERICA

I see the joy and true meaning of Christmas whenever I look into Gracen Seabaugh's eyes.

Contents

Foreword

IF YOU WERE TO ASK MY CLOSEST FRIENDS what are the most important things in my life, most would likely say, "The Lord, her family, and then her books." I am a voracious reader. It would not be an exaggeration to say that reading is central to who I am and is at the core of my being.

If you were to look at my bookshelves, you would find a wide variety of titles and authors. I even collect signed first editions. But as you search my personal library, an author that pops up again and again is Ace Collins. I deeply enjoy his work, but what fascinates me most about Ace is that his writing is so eclectic. His work ranges from history to biography to devotionals to novels, and in those pages he has introduced me to a plethora of fascinating people and stimulating facts. Yet, even though his books are so varied, there is always a theme that stays consistent in each. No matter the genre, Ace subtly encourages his readers to look out not in, to grow rather than stagnate, and to get involved to make a lasting impact.

When I look back at my own career, I realize, like Ace, I'm pretty eclectic too. When I performed I constantly worked gospel, blues, rock, R & B, and country into my repertoire. Yet it was during the holidays when I had the most freedom to employ music from across the spectrum. Thus, one of my favorite recording projects was my Christmas album. For me, that experience allowed me to become

fully immersed in the myriad emotions that make December the most wonderful time of the year.

Perhaps my love of Christmas is why I am so drawn to this book. Inside the pages of *The Most Wonderful Time of the Year* are things you can cook, gifts you can make, and stories behind the songs that set the holidays to music. And while each of these elements is entertaining, what I most treasure about this project are the thirty-one devotionals. In these daily readings are deep and profound spiritual elements, and in the carefully crafted words are practical lessons you will recall and cherish long after Christmas has come and gone. I also love that this is an optimistic book that inspires as it informs. It spotlights not just the birth of Christ but the purpose for His life. Perhaps, most importantly, these daily devotionals connect Christmas to Easter and Jesus's birth to His resurrection as they challenge us to live more like Christ all year long.

The Most Wonderful Time of the Year is a special treat that will illuminate your holidays and make them more meaningful. It is a book you will likely bring out each Christmas and read again and again. I also think it is one you will want to share with others. I know I will.

Have a merry and powerful Christmas, and may the Lord's grace touch your heart with the wonder of the season.

Barbara Mandrell

December 1

It Is a Wonderful Life

The angel said, "Don't be afraid! Look! I bring good news to you—
wonderful, joyous news for all people. Your savior is born today in
David's city. He is Christ the Lord."

LUKE 2:10-11

FOR MILLIONS, CHRISTMAS IS NOT CHRISTMAS until they view the 1946 Frank Capra film *It's A Wonderful Life.* In this Hollywood classic, George Bailey sees what the world would have been like had he not been born. When faced with what might have been, George discovers that the world would have been a far darker place without him.

A thousand years ago, advent was a time of personal introspection. One element of the tradition centered on how different the world would be if there had been no Jesus. As we begin embracing this new Christmas season, perhaps, to put things into the proper perspective, we first need to visualize a world where Christ was never born.

For starters there would be no cards, no lights, no decorations, no "Silent Night" or "White Christmas," no shopping, no gifts, and no family gatherings. December 25th would be just another day on the calendar, and the wonder and joy of this season would be something we would never experience. Yet that is just the beginning.

Your salvation would not be anchored on grace but on the law. The church where you attended as a child, the place where you were saved, the building where you now gather with family would have never been constructed. The relationships you built in church would also be lost. There would be no church bells, no "Amazing Grace," and no chance for redemption. The billions who have been touched through the gifts and missions of the church would have never felt the love of Christ. The compassion born of faith would be completely unknown.

Without Christ there would have been no Mother Teresa, Albert Schweitzer, Martin Luther, Lottie Moon, or Billy Graham. The purpose for their great work would have not been there to motivate or inspire them.

It is easy to get overwhelmed with the demands of the season and fall into the trap of dreading the holidays. Fighting the crowds at the mall, decorating the house, wrapping the gifts, and meeting all the holiday obligations is never easy, but consider the alternative. If there were no reason for Christmas then, just like Bedford Falls without the influence of George Bailey, our world would be a much darker and depressing place. Christmas celebrates not just the birth of Christ but how Jesus changed the world and changed each of us. That dramatic change is one we should embrace on the day we kick off this month of joy as well as on each day of our lives! Yes—because of the wonderful life Jesus has given to this world and to each of us—there is a reason to celebrate! Because of Christ, there is not only a Christmas but also hope, light, and joy on each day of the year!

Angels from the Realms of Glory

IRISH-BORN JAMES MONTGOMERY WAS one of the leading voices for Irish independence. As the publisher of the *Sheffield Iris*, his fiery words landed him in prison several times. On December 24, 1816, Montgomery turned from revolution to inspiration and penned "Angels from the Realms of Glory." Set to music by an Englishman, Montgomery's poem would become one of the first Christmas songs ever sung in an Anglican church. In the end, the revolution the Irish Catholic writer started did not free Ireland, but it did open the Church of England to using Christmas music in worship services.

Angels from the realms of glory,
wing your flight o'er all the earth;
Ye who sang creation's story
now proclaim Messiah's birth:
Come and worship, come and worship,
worship Christ, the newborn King.

Shepherds, in the fields abiding,
watching o'er your flocks by night,
God with us is now residing;
yonder shines the infant light:

3

Come and worship, come and worship,
worship Christ, the newborn King.

Sages, leave your contemplations,
brighter visions beam afar;
Seek the great Desire of nations;
ye have seen his natal star:
Come and worship, come and worship,
worship Christ, the newborn King.

Saints, before the altar bending,
watching long in hope and fear;
Suddenly the Lord, descending,
in his temple shall appear:
Come and worship, come and worship,
worship Christ, the newborn King.

Pamper the One You Love!

If you are looking for a practical gift this holiday season, why don't you make a recipe ring using all of the amazing recipes in this book, or maybe some of your family's favorites?

Recipe Ring

> 4 x 6 blank note or recipe cards
> colored paper
> printer, pen, or marker
> laminator
> hole punch
> metal binder ring
> new wooden spatula (with a hole in end of handle)

Begin by writing your favorite recipes on pretty recipe cards or by printing them out on plain paper with the margins small enough to fit on the 4 x 6 card. Once printed, cut them out and glue them to the colored paper. (You could use different colors for different sections.) Then, glue the colored paper to the note card. Organize the recipes by sections (entrées, sides, desserts, beverages, and so on). If possible, laminate the cards to protect them from wear and tear. Using a hole punch, punch a hole in the cards and add them to the ring. Attach the ring of recipe cards to the hole in the end of the spatula. Wrap and give as a lovely gift!

December 2

Cherishing the Past

*When the angels returned to heaven, the shepherds said to each other,
"Let's go right now to Bethlehem and see what's happened. Let's
confirm what the Lord has revealed to us." They went quickly and
found Mary and Joseph, and the baby lying in the manger. When
they saw this, they reported what they had been told about this child.
Everyone who heard it was amazed at what the shepherds told them.
Mary committed these things to memory and considered them carefully.
The shepherds returned home, glorifying and praising God for all they
had heard and seen. Everything happened just as they had been told.*

LUKE 2:15-20

LUKE WRITES ABOUT MARY CONCENTRATING on the aspects of the
first Christmas and imprinting those moments deeply into her mind.
This intimate gospel record proves the mother of Jesus treasured and
understood the full importance of each visitor, word, and gift. These
memories likely offered her great joy and comfort as the years passed.

In 1937 Ralph Rainger and Leo Robin penned an Academy
Award–winning song, "Thanks for the Memory," that premiered in
a motion picture that is now all but forgotten and was introduced
by a man never really considered a vocalist. This song became an
American classic and the theme song for comedian Bob Hope. The

warm memories Hope created through decades of entertaining men and women in uniform would come to make this number special for millions who had never seen the movie *The Big Broadcast of 1938*. And because Hope's tours usually happened during the holiday season, many still associate "Thanks for the Memory" with Christmas.

Each December offers a return of cherished traditions and songs as well as the renewal of greetings between friends and family. In that way, Christmas is a time machine where a lyric, a photo, an ornament, or a card can bring into sharp focus a special moment from our past.

What are the personal memories you are thankful for? What are the treasured elements of past holidays that warm your heart? As the Christmas music returns, it is once more time to hear the voices from yesterday, feel the love of those who were part of Christmas past, and celebrate with the joy and wonder of times when those memories were made.

As you begin your celebration of this season, take time to embrace recollections of your past holidays and once more bask in the joys of Christmas past. If you push yourself deep enough into your memories of parents, grandparents, friends, school plays, or church pageants, you might suddenly feel the innocent wonder of the season that made your childhood Christmases come alive.

Christmas has always been about giving, so once you are immersed in holiday memories, call someone who shared one of those special moments with you. By doing so you are spreading the joy of holidays past and setting the mood to build a wonderful foundation for this new Christmas season. Yes, it is time to be thankful for the memories.

Hark! The Herald Angels Sing

When writing the lyrics to "Hark! The Herald Angels Sing," Charles Wesley embraced an Old English term that correctly quoted the biblical narrative of Jesus's birth found in Luke 2:13-14. In the carol's original form, the title was "Hark! How All the Welkin Rings." *Welkin* is defined as when the vault of heaven makes a loud noise. When the music publisher changed *welkin* to *angels*, Wesley was livid because he felt the song was no longer biblically correct. Today, thanks to George Whitefield's edits, most have forgotten about the role of the welkin.

Hark! the herald angels sing,
"Glory to the newborn King;
Peace on earth, and mercy mild,
God and sinners reconciled!"
Joyful, all ye nations, rise,
join the triumph of the skies;
With th'angelic hosts proclaim,
"Christ is born in Bethlehem!"
Hark! the herald angels sing,
"Glory to the newborn King."

Christ, by highest heaven adored,
Christ, the everlasting Lord;

Late in time behold him come,
offspring of a virgin's womb.
Veiled in flesh the Godhead see;
hail th'incarnate Deity,
Pleased with us in flesh to dwell,
Jesus, our Emmanuel.
Hark! the herald angels sing,
"Glory to the newborn King."

Hail the heaven-born Prince of Peace!
Hail the Sun of Righteousness!
Light and life to all he brings,
risen with healing in his wings.
Mild he lays his glory by,
born that we no more may die,
Born to raise us from the earth,
born to give us second birth.
Hark! the herald angels sing,
"Glory to the newborn King."

Feed the One You Love!

These delicious buttery shortbread cookies have just the slightest bit of orange zest, a small amount of finely chopped pecans, and delicious holiday sugar plum jam. Your entire family will love them! They are perfect for any Christmas brunch, dessert, cookie exchange, or homemade gift.

Sugar Plum Shortbread Christmas Cookies

> 2½ cups all-purpose flour
> ½ tsp. ground cinnamon
> ¼ tsp. freshly grated whole nutmeg
> ¼ cup finely chopped toasted pecans
> 6 Tbsp. granulated sugar
> 1½ Tbsp. freshly grated orange zest
> 1 cup salted butter, cut into small bits
> Stonewall Kitchen Sugar Plum Jam, strained
> granulated sugar (for sprinkling)
> sparkling white sugar (for sprinkling)

Arrange the oven rack in the lower third of the oven and preheat to 325 degrees. Line a baking sheet with parchment paper or a silicone baking mat; set aside. In a medium bowl, combine flour, spices, pecans, sugar, and orange zest. Using a pastry blender, or heavy-duty stand mixer with paddle attachment on low speed, add the butter until the mixture resembles fine crumbs and starts to cling together. The dough will still be very crumbly. Knead until smooth. Form into a ball and then flatten slightly. On a lightly floured work surface, roll the dough until it is a half-inch thick. Using 1½- to 3-inch size cookie cutters, cut into desired shapes. Place on prepared baking sheets 2 inches apart. Bake for 18-22 minutes (18-20 minutes for small cookies or 20-22 minutes for large cookies) or until the bottoms start to brown and the centers are set. Allow the cookies to cool slightly on baking sheets for 2 minutes. Using a metal cookie spatula, transfer the cookies to wire racks to cool completely before icing them with jam and sprinkling them with sugars.

Makes 16-18 shortbread cookies

December 3

When Christmas Is Near

In those days Caesar Augustus declared that everyone throughout
the empire should be enrolled in the tax lists. This first enrollment
occurred when Quirinius governed Syria. Everyone went to their
own cities to be enrolled. Since Joseph belonged to David's house and
family line, he went up from the city of Nazareth in Galilee to
David's city, called Bethlehem, in Judea.

LUKE 2:1-4

WHY DO WE KNOW ABOUT JESUS'S BIRTH? Why are we aware that
Mary and Joseph went to Bethlehem? Why, some twenty centuries
later, can we read the writings of Paul, Timothy, and James? It is
because those who witnessed the events took the time to write down
what they saw and heard.

In 1959, Jesse Hollis and Clyde Otis took their thoughts of Christmas and placed them into a song. With its scenes of snowy nights,
evergreens, caroling choirs, and anxious children, "This Time of the
Year When Christmas Is Near" captures the holidays in Norman
Rockwell detail. In its simply stated but profound lyrics, it notes
what those in a holiday rush often miss but should treasure. In that
way it brings Christmas into sharp focus.

As a college student Shelby Seabaugh wrote short notes about things she saw that inspired, moved, or blessed her. After recording those observations she dropped them into a box to save. The energetic, optimistic, and outgoing coed died tragically when she was twenty. When retrieving Shelby's personal belongings from her dorm room, her parents found the box filled with her "blessings." These hundreds of notes gave them a deeper insight into their daughter's faith and compassion, motivating them to look out into the world and note the joy and wonder that most miss and almost no one records.

On a daily basis you need to pause and take note of moments that lift your spirits and touch your heart, and then write those observations down. When you find yourself overcome with obligations and deadlines and you feel as though you are drowning in stress, you can look back at what you've written and be reminded of the blessings that are all around you during this time of the year. Suddenly life is once more in perspective because there is no better stress reliever than counting blessings.

Shelby did something else that you might want to incorporate into this holiday season. When she noted people unselfishly doing something for others or using their talents to bless those around them, she wrote thank-you notes and anonymously sent them as a way to encourage those givers to keep giving and serving.

Around you right now are friends and neighbors who are giving their time, energy, and talents to lift others. Whether they realize it or not, they are modeling Christ through these selfless actions. As a way of honoring those who recorded the life of Jesus, why not take a

few moments this holiday season to write down what you've observed and share that good news with those who have inspired you? Your written words will likely remain with them for much longer than just the Christmas season; in fact, they might just last a lifetime. Such is the power of the written word.

There's a Song in the Air

"There's a Song in the Air" was all but lost for three decades. Published as a poem in a book that sold few copies, Josiah Holland's inspired prose describing the birth of Jesus as a new song might have languished in obscurity if Karl Harrington had not been given the task of assembling a new Methodist Hymnal in 1904. On a hot summer day, decades after Holland had died, Harrington read the poem and composed music to finally compete this timeless carol.

There's a song in the air!
There's a star in the sky!
There's a mother's deep prayer
and a baby's low cry!
And the star rains its fire
while the beautiful sing,
For the manger of Bethlehem
cradles a King!

There's a tumult of joy
o'er the wonderful birth,
For the virgin's sweet boy
is the Lord of the earth.
Ay! the star rains its fire

15

while the beautiful sing,
For the manger of Bethlehem
cradles a King!

In the light of that star
lie the ages impearled;
And that song from afar
has swept over the world.
Every hearth is aflame,
and the beautiful sing
In the homes of the nations
that Jesus is King!

We rejoice in the light,
and we echo the song
That comes down through the night
from the heavenly throng.
Ay! we shout to the lovely
evangel they bring,
And we greet in his cradle
our Savior and King!

Pamper the One You Love!

With so much going on during the holiday season, who doesn't need a good foot soak? This recipe is meant specifically for your tootsies! As an added benefit, the Lime Mint Foot Scrub is known to relieve foot pain by boosting overall circulation.

Lime Mint Foot Scrub

> 2 cups Epsom salt
> ½ cup baking soda
> zest of one lime
> 3-4 drops lime essential oil
> 3-4 drops peppermint essential oil
> green food coloring (optional)
> quart-size glass jar or bag

In a large bowl, combine the Epsom salt, baking soda, and the lime zest with a wooden spoon. After it is mixed thoroughly, add the lime and peppermint essential oils. If desired, add a drop or two of green food coloring. Place the mixture into a glass jar or bag and decorate with twine or ribbon.

December 4

Putting Gifts into Perspective

When they heard the king, they went; and look, the star they had seen in the east went ahead of them until it stood over the place where the child was. When they saw the star, they were filled with joy. They entered the house and saw the child with Mary his mother. Falling to their knees, they honored him. Then they opened their treasure chests and presented him with gifts of gold, frankincense, and myrrh.

MATTHEW 2:9-11

ONE OF THE VERY OLDEST HOLIDAY TRADITIONS is the one many dislike the most—the giving of gifts. Trying to find just the right present for each person on your list can be mind-boggling. Therefore, before beginning the actual task of shopping, you need to get into the mode of thinking like a wise man. That requires looking into the hearts and minds of those early givers.

Those we call the kings from the Orient brought three unique gifts to the baby Jesus. On first glance none seems suited for an infant. Yet, as we understand the era and what this baby would become, the gifts were perfect.

At the time of Christ's birth, gold was only given to a loved one or a person of very high standing. Thus, the giver must have realized the child born in a stable was destined to become a king. The frankincense tree was considered so sacred that only those pure of heart and mind were allowed to come near it. The oil made from the sap of this tree was used during special religious offerings. This giver must somehow have known the baby was to become a man who would minister to the needs of the world. Myrrh was a rare and expensive resin used in burial ceremonies. The giver of this gift somehow realized this child would one day lay down His life for all of humankind.

The visitors from the East gave more than just three physical gifts; they also gave their time. Sacrificing moments from your life to honor someone else through attention and devotion is one of the greatest presents you can give. Just as these men did this for Christ, you can do it for others. There are many around you who hunger for a visitor bearing nothing but a few minutes of conversation. To them your time is the greatest gift of all.

There is an old saying, "It's the thought, not the gift, that counts," but the wise men seem to prove that the thought and the gift actually work hand in hand. If you think not in the short term but consider the entirety of a person's life, you can likely find a gift that will become a treasured memory. But how do you gain the wisdom for this kind of choice? For those who brought the first presents to Jesus, it likely began with prayer. So maybe this is the year you need to pray over your list before you actually do the shopping. Perhaps then you will have the insight to do honor to one of our oldest Christmas traditions and bless others as they have never been blessed before.

We Three Kings

Just four years before the Civil War, John Henry Hopkins Jr., an Episcopal priest with degrees from both the University of Vermont and New York Law School, decided to write a song as an Epiphany gift for his nieces and nephews. In order to simplify the lyrics, he opted to have a wise man for each of the three gifts given to the baby Jesus. The clergyman later published his carol in a hymnal. In the 1870s, when "We Three Kings" became a popular anthem for children's choirs and carolers, it literally rewrote history. Because of this carol, most seem to believe there were three wise men when in fact the Bible does not note how many visitors came from the East.

We three kings of Orient are;
bearing gifts we traverse afar,
Field and fountain, moor and mountain,
following yonder star.

O Star of wonder, star of light,
star with royal beauty bright,
Westward leading, still proceeding,
guide us to thy perfect light.

Born a King on Bethlehem's plain,
gold I bring to crown him again,

King forever, ceasing never,
over us all to reign.

O Star of wonder, star of light,
star with royal beauty bright,
Westward leading, still proceeding,
guide us to thy perfect light.

Frankincense to offer have I;
incense owns a Deity nigh;
Prayer and praising, voices raising,
worshiping God on high.

O Star of wonder, star of light,
star with royal beauty bright,
Westward leading, still proceeding,
guide us to thy perfect light.

Myrrh is mine; its bitter perfume
breathes of life of gathering gloom;
Sorrowing, sighing, bleeding, dying,
sealed in the stone-cold tomb.

O Star of wonder, star of light,
star with royal beauty bright,
Westward leading, still proceeding,
guide us to thy perfect light.

Glorious now behold Him arise;
King and God and sacrifice:
Alleluia, Alleluia
sounds through the earth and skies.

O Star of wonder, star of light,
star with royal beauty bright,
Westward leading, still proceeding,
guide us to thy perfect light.

Feed the One You Love!

If crispy coconut cookies are one of your favorite treats, then this recipe is perfect for you. They also make the perfect cookie to give to others.

Coconut Thins

> ¼ cup butter
>
> ⅓ cup light brown sugar
>
> 2½ Tbsp. golden or corn syrup
>
> 6½ Tbsp. all-purpose flour
>
> ½ tsp. lemon juice
>
> 2 Tbsp. shredded coconut

Preheat the oven to 350 degrees. Line four baking sheets with parchment paper or silicone baking mats; set aside. Pour butter, sugar, and syrup into a small, heavy-based pan. Heat gently about 10 minutes over a low heat until the butter has melted and the sugar has dissolved. Leave the mixture to cool slightly, about 2-3 minutes, then sift in the flour. Pour in the lemon juice and stir well to mix thoroughly. Drop 1½ tablespoons of the mixture onto each of the prepared baking trays to make neat circles, about 4 inches apart. Sprinkle a small amount of coconut onto each drop. Bake for about 10-15 minutes, or until the mixture is spread out well, lacey in appearance, and a dark golden color. Once baked, quickly remove the

cookies from the oven and sprinkle a very small amount of coconut over them. Leave them on the baking tray until firm, and then transfer them to a cooling rack.

Makes 14 cookies

December 5

Time to Empty the Trash

More than anything you guard, protect your mind,
for life flows from it.

PROVERBS 4:23

A FRIEND ONCE ASKED ME WHO WAS THE most important person in my life. I rattled off a long list of people, starting with family then moving to my friends, pastor, doctor, lawyer, and neighbor. After assuring me that I was the most positive, upbeat person she had ever met, she informed me the most important person in my life was the garbage collector. Why? Because if the garbage collector quit coming to my house, my trash would start rotting, and with that decay, rodents and insects would move in. In that kind of a world, it would be all but impossible to maintain a positive attitude.

Often, during the busy holiday season, our lives get so cluttered we begin to lose perspective. When it seems as though the demands are overwhelming our time and energy, our mood dramatically changes. We are easily frustrated and impatient, we lash out without provocation, and we tend to look upon the world as if it is out to get us.

Imagine for a moment the plight of Joseph and Mary. As they looked forward to Jesus's birth, the government of Rome forced them

out of their home and onto the highway. The fact that a baby was on the way did not matter. The roads were likely covered with people rushing to meet their obligation for the census. Inns were packed, as were places to eat. It was likely a time when people were impatient and rude. Visualize being a pregnant woman and battling this type of situation. What would your attitude have been?

From what the Bible tells us about Mary, she was well versed in scripture. Therefore she fully understood the charge in Proverbs to protect her mind. To accomplish this Mary likely threw away all her mental garbage. That way she could reflect the patience, compassion, and love of the God who had called her to bear His Son.

As destructive as holding onto our physical garbage can be, clinging to the mental garbage carries even a greater risk. It not only affects our attitudes toward those around us, but it defines us to the world. So how do we get rid of this mental trash? Like Mary did: we give it to God through prayer.

Prayer allows us to put things into perspective. It gives us the ability to forgive and move forward. It also permits us to sift through what is important and throw away that which is not.

Don't get so busy during the holiday season that you forget to pray. Cling to those prayers as a way to keep your mind clear. With the mental garbage gone, you will be able to handle all you need to do in a way that will reflect the joy that each of us wants to feel during this season. And don't forget, no matter how many things you have on your plate, compared to Mary, you've got it easy.

O Come, All Ye Faithful

When Columbia Records produced the very first electronic recording on March 31, 1925, the company featured a Christmas carol written by a Catholic priest in 1750. One of the best-known holiday anthems, "O Come All Ye Faithful," initially landed on the American pop charts in 1905, thus becoming one of the very first Christmas songs to make the top ten. Yet it was the 1925 version, recorded with the newly developed electric microphones, that established this carol as a chart topper. Recorded by thousands of members of American glee clubs on the stage of the New York Metropolitan Opera, this carol would signal the transformation of the recording industry and become one of the most successful records of its era.

O come, all ye faithful,
joyful and triumphant,
O come ye, O come ye, to Bethlehem.
Come and behold him,
born the King of angels;
O come, let us adore him,
O come, let us adore him,
O come, let us adore him,
Christ the Lord.

True God of true God,
Light from Light Eternal,
lo, he shuns not
the virgin's womb;
Son of the Father,
begotten, not created;
O come, let us adore him,
O come, let us adore him,
O come, let us adore him,
Christ the Lord.

Sing, choirs of angels,
sing in exultation;
O sing, all ye citizens of heaven above!
Glory to God,
all glory in the highest;
O come, let us adore him,
O come, let us adore him,
O come, let us adore him,
Christ the Lord.

See how the shepherds,
summoned to his cradle,
leaving their flocks,
draw nigh to gaze;
we too will tither
bend our joyful footsteps.

O come, let us adore him,
O come, let us adore him,
O come, let us adore him,
Christ the Lord.

Child, for us sinners
poor and in the manger,
we would embrace thee
with love and awe.
Who would not love thee,
loving us so dearly?
O come, let us adore him,
O come, let us adore him,
O come, let us adore him,
Christ the Lord.

Yea, Lord, we greet thee,
born this happy morning,
Jesus, to thee be
all glory given.
Word of the Father,
now in flesh appearing:
O come, let us adore him,
O come, let us adore him,
O come, let us adore him,
Christ the Lord.

Pamper the One You Love!

With all the stress of the Christmas season, why not give a gift of rest and relaxation, either to someone you love, or for your own well-being? Therapeutic bath salts are perfect for that long soak in the tub, and it's also commonly known that Epsom salts improve heart health and circulation.

Lavender Bath Salts in a Jar

> 2 cups Epsom salt
> ¾ cup baking soda
> 6-10 drops lavender essential oil
> ¼ cup dried lavender (optional)
> quart-size glass jar
> washi tape

Mix the ingredients well in a medium-sized glass bowl. Let the salt dry overnight. While the salt is drying, decorate the jar with washi tape. It's easy to make a fun and festive Christmas tree design by placing strips of tape in various sizes to the jar. Once it's designed, add the Lavender Bath Salts.

December 6

The Importance of Encouragement

A child is born to us, a son is given to us,
and authority will be on his shoulders.
He will be named
Wonderful Counselor, Mighty God,
Eternal Father, Prince of Peace.
There will be vast authority and endless peace
for David's throne and for his kingdom,
establishing and sustaining it
with justice and righteousness
now and forever.

ISAIAH 9:6-7

FOR MANY THE GREATEST CHRISTIAN composition is *Messiah*. This oratorio, written by the legendary George Frideric Handel, does more than set to music the life of the One whose birth is celebrated during this season; it fully defines what Christ should mean to each of us. Yet it is only because of the desire of one man to lift the spirits of another that this musical exists. That story of faith is almost as powerful as the song itself.

In August, 1741, fifty-six-year-old George Handel was at the end of his rope. In poor health, the once famous composer was living alone and suffering from nightmares of spending his final days on earth in a debtor's prison. As the bills mounted, it seemed all the man had left were his prayers. A drowning person will cling to even the smallest of hopes, and when an old friend asked the down-and-out composer to conduct an orchestra for a charity event, Handel jumped at the opportunity. He accepted the invitation not as a way of rebuilding his career, but so he could leave London and escape his creditors.

As Handel planned for the trip, he received a letter from another friend. In this correspondence Charles Jennens explained an idea for a new oratorio. Jennens reduced the Old Testament and New Testament stories of Christ to those passages he viewed as the most important and challenged Handel to put them to music. Inspired by Jennens's faith in his abilities, the all-but-forgotten composer spent twenty-four days writing what would become the most familiar oratorio of all time. He later told friends that when he completed the famous "Hallelujah Chorus," he thought he saw "all Heaven before me, and the great God himself."

Since its debut, Handel's *Messiah* has been used to raise money for millions who were at the end of their ropes. Perhaps most fitting is that the song's composer was the first to be lifted out of poverty and despair by this musical masterpiece.

So what can we learn from the story of *Messiah*? If Charles Jennens had not shared a letter with George Handel, there would have been no inspiration for the music. When the world had written the composer off, Jennens did not. He still believed in his old friend, and this caused Handel to once more believe in himself.

Now is the time for us to be like Charles Jennens. We need to look for those suffering in darkness and despair and touch them with faith, hope, and love. This simple act of compassion could restore some joy to a hopeless person's holidays or maybe even be the motivation for something far greater.

Hallelujah Chorus

In 1742, on the second night *Messiah* was performed in London, King George II attended the concert. With George Handel directing and with a full house in attendance, London buzzed with excitement, and enthusiastic applause greeted each new element of the production. When the concert progressed to the oratorio's signature piece, the king was so overcome with emotion that after only a few notes, he stood, initiating a tradition that continues to this day. When choirs sing the "Hallelujah Chorus," people still stand to acknowledge the power of the work as well as our Lord, whom Handel honored with his greatest composition.

Hallelujah! Hallelujah!
Hallelujah! Hallelujah! Hallelujah!
For the Lord God omnipotent reigneth;
Hallelujah! Hallelujah!
Hallelujah! Hallelujah! Hallelujah!
For the Lord God omnipotent reigneth.
Hallelujah! Hallelujah! Hallelujah! Hallelujah!
For the Lord God omnipotent reigneth.
Hallelujah! Hallelujah!
Hallelujah! Hallelujah! Hallelujah!
Hallelujah! Hallelujah!

Hallelujah! Hallelujah! Hallelujah!
Hallelujah! Hallelujah!
Hallelujah! Hallelujah! Hallelujah!
The kingdom of this world is become
The kingdom of our Lord, and of His Christ,
and of His Christ.
And He shall reign forever and ever,
King of kings,
and Lord of lords.
King of kings,
and Lord of lords.
King of kings,
and Lord of lords, and Lord of lords,
And He shall reign, and He shall reign forever
    and ever,
forever and ever,
Hallelujah! Hallelujah!
And He shall reign forever and ever,
forever and ever.
And He shall reign forever and ever,
King of kings!
and Lord of lords!
Hallelujah! Hallelujah!
Hallelujah! Hallelujah! Hallelujah!

Feed the One You Love!

Pecan Snowball Cookies are the perfect classic treat for your holiday cookie platter. These buttery, melt-in-your-mouth shortbread cookies have just enough chopped pecans to make you go nuts!

Pecan Snowball Cookies

> 1 cup unsalted butter, softened
>
> 1 cup powdered sugar
>
> 1 tsp. vanilla extract
>
> 2¼ cups all-purpose flour
>
> 1 cup finely chopped pecans

Preheat the oven to 350 degrees. Line a baking sheet with parchment paper or a silicone baking mat; set aside. Using a stand mixer or hand mixer, cream butter and ½ cup sugar together until light and fluffy. Add vanilla and add flour slowly; mix until just combined. Fold in chopped pecans. Beat at low speed (scraping bowl as necessary) until mixed well. Cover the cookie dough with plastic wrap and chill for at least 30 minutes. Roll the dough into 2-tablespoon-sized dough balls. Place on the prepared baking pan about 2 inches apart. Repeat until all the dough is used. Bake the cookies for 14-15 minutes, or until the bottoms are just slightly brown. Be careful not to overbake. Remove from the oven and cool on the baking pan for about 2 minutes or until you can handle them with your hands. Sift ½ cup sugar into a medium bowl. While the cookies are still warm, roll them in the powdered sugar. Place the cookies on a cooling rack. Once they have cooled completely, roll them one final time in the powdered sugar.

Makes 16 cookies

December 7

Vision

Jesus entered Jericho and was passing through town. A man there named Zacchaeus, a ruler among tax collectors, was rich. He was trying to see who Jesus was, but, being a short man, he couldn't because of the crowd. So he ran ahead and climbed up a sycamore tree so he could see Jesus, who was about to pass that way. When Jesus came to that spot, he looked up and said, "Zacchaeus, come down at once. I must stay in your home today." So Zacchaeus came down at once, happy to welcome Jesus. Everyone who saw this grumbled, saying, "He has gone to be the guest of a sinner." Zacchaeus stopped and said to the Lord, "Look, Lord, I give half of my possessions to the poor. And if I have cheated anyone, I repay them four times as much." Jesus said to him, "Today, salvation has come to this household because he too is a son of Abraham. The Human One came to seek and save the lost."

LUKE 19:1-10

ONE OF THE MOST BEAUTIFUL MODERN SECULAR Christmas carols was written by master country song scribe Willie Nelson. Nelson, who spent years struggling as a musician and songwriter before making it big, was a man who could identify with poverty. When he came to Nashville in search of a career, he spent a decade hungry and sometimes homeless. He sold the two major hits he penned during those lean days for a few hundred dollars just to pay bills. Those songs would eventually garner millions of dollars in royalties that Nelson would never see.

One of the things great songwriters have to have is vision. That means they often view the world in slow motion or stop action. So when things are a blur for most of us, they focus on the things we miss. Such was the case when Nelson wrote "Pretty Paper." On the surface it seems like a love song, but if you really listen to the lyrics, you understand Nelson is pointing out the plight of a hopeless man, living on the streets, who remains all but invisible to the people rushing through their holiday adventures. Ultimately "Pretty Paper" is a tragic story of good people too busy to stop and help someone in need.

On the day Christ spotted Zacchaeus, thousands of people were crying out for Jesus to notice them. Most of us would have overlooked the man in the tree, but even with all the demands being placed upon Him, Jesus saw Zacchaeus. The lesson of that day should still resonate with us.

At Christmas, like no other time of the year, we have a multitude of demands pulling us in myriad directions. We have presents to buy, gifts to wrap, decorations to put up, food to prepare, and parties to attend, but our demands are no excuse for not taking a few moments to notice those who are lonely, hungry, hopeless, and in need.

In Nelson's "Pretty Paper" there is a line, "Should you stop? Better not, much too busy." Don't embrace that as your motto this holiday season. These are the moments to not get so caught up in the pretty paper we miss the opportunity to be like Christ. Now is the time to open your eyes to both the wonder and the needs found at Christmas.

ACE COLLINS

It Came Upon the Midnight Clear

In 1849, Harvard-educated Edmund H. Sears was a concerned and depressed pastor. As he looked ahead to Christmas, he was deeply disappointed by the lack of generosity he saw in America. Too many people were poor and hungry, and too few people seemed to care. To fully state the nature of Christ and underscore what was expected of Christians he penned the poem "It Came Upon the Midnight Clear." The message he presented was a challenge to those in his congregation to actually display Jesus's spirit through acts of kindness.

It came upon the midnight clear,
that glorious song of old,
From angels bending near the earth,
to touch their harps of gold:
"Peace on the earth, good will to men
from heaven's all gracious King."
The world in solemn stillness lay,
to hear the angels sing.

Still through the cloven skies they come
with peaceful wings unfurled,
And still their heavenly music floats
o'er all the weary world;

Above its sad and lowly plains,
they bend on hovering wing,
And ever o'er its Babel sounds
the blessed angels sing.

And ye, beneath life's crushing load,
whose forms are bending low,
Who toil along the climbing way
with painful steps and slow,
Look now! for glad and golden hours
come swiftly on the wing.
O rest beside the weary road,
and hear the angels sing!

For lo! the days are hastening on,
by prophets seen of old,
When with the ever-circling years
shall come the time foretold
When peace shall over all the earth
its ancient splendors fling,
And the whole world send back the song
which now the angels sing.

Pamper the One You Love!

If you are considering making a spa gift basket using the Lime Mint Foot Scrub and Lavender Bath Salts, why not add some Lavender Lemon Soap? Your loved one will appreciate all of the homemade gifts!

Lavender Lemon Soap

>2 pounds goat's milk soap base
>10-15 drops lavender essential oil
>purple soap dye (optional)
>soap mold
>rubbing alcohol in small spray bottle
>5-6 drops lemon essential oil
>burlap
>twine

In a double boiler, divide the soap base in half. Melt one pound of soap for 15-20 minutes, or until completely liquefied. Stir in 10-15 drops of lavender essential oil. If desired, add in a few drops of purple soap dye to add color. Pour into soap molds and lightly spray alcohol on top to eliminate bubbles. Allow soap layer to harden for at least one hour. Melt remaining soap and add lemon essential oil. Pour over lavender soap layer and allow it to harden for 1-2 hours before removing. Decorate the soap bars by wrapping them in a thin strip of burlap tied with twine.

December 8

Worry Is a Thief

"Peace I leave with you. My peace I give you. I give to you not as the world gives. Don't be troubled or afraid."

JOHN 14:27

JUST AS THE HOLIDAYS BRING OUT JOY and wonder, they also seem to deliver feelings of inadequacy. Long before Santa makes his rounds, the Grinch is in our midst bringing insecurity and worry.

In 1941 one of the world's most accomplished artists went into a meeting feeling as if he had failed his assignment. As he met with the star of the motion picture he'd been contracted to score, Irving Berlin began with an apology. Even before he sat down at the piano to share the music he had penned for *Holiday Inn*, Berlin explained that his work was not up to the standards of a Bing Crosby musical.

Born in Russia and brought to America as a child by a family seeking religious freedom, Berlin composed more hit songs that any writer of his generation. His ability to connect his lyrics with listeners was unparalleled. Simply put, he was in a class by himself. Yet on this day what Berlin really wanted was more time. He had toiled for weeks on a Christmas song only to come up with something he viewed as second rate. But even though the songwriter tried to beg off, Crosby

demanded to hear the "inadequate" holiday offering. As Berlin finished playing, he apologized again and assured Crosby if given a bit more time he could come up with something better. Crosby shook his head and smiled, saying he liked "White Christmas" just as it was.

Introduced on Crosby's Christmas 1941 radio show, the song would quickly emerge as the most popular recording of all time. Embraced by people all over the globe, it became the holiday anthem for a world at war as well as a Christmas standard during peace. The song that Berlin felt was inadequate is today recognized as his greatest work.

Worry robs us of joy and peace. At Christmas much of our worry centers on not being able to find just the right present or the right words. Feelings of inadequacy keep us from volunteering for parts in community or church programs. Doubt prevents us from sharing our talents and spiritual gifts with others. Simply put, we are afraid that what we have purchased, made, said, or presented is not good enough.

If we truly believe that the Son of God was born on Christmas, if we believe that Jesus paid for our sins on a cross and rose from the grave, and if we believe that in Him all things are possible, then what is holding us back from the joy of this season? The spirit that you welcomed into your soul when you accepted Christ wants to be released. It wants a chance to shine. Don't let your human frailties keep you from sharing your heart and inspiration this holiday season. What you are so afraid of as being not good enough might be just what someone else needs to receive. So pray, let God shine, do your best, and don't keep worry from letting you enjoy a "white Christmas."

God Rest Ye Merry, Gentlemen

During the Middle Ages, when this song was written, the word *rest* had several meanings that are no longer commonly used. Thus this old carol often confuses many Christians. After all, why would God want happy people to sleep? Rather than resting shouldn't we be out doing His work? This song's writer likely meant for *rest* to mean "make" or "keep." When *rest* is replaced in that fashion this holiday song suddenly has a very powerful message.

God rest ye merry, gentlemen, let nothing you dismay,
Remember, Christ our Savior was born on
    Christmas Day;
To save us all from Satan's power when we were
    gone astray.
O tidings of comfort and joy, comfort and joy;
O tidings of comfort and joy.

In Bethlehem, in Israel, this blessed Babe was born,
And laid within a manger upon this blessed morn;
The which His mother Mary did nothing take in scorn.
O tidings of comfort and joy, comfort and joy;
O tidings of comfort and joy.

From God our heavenly Father a blessed angel came;
And unto certain shepherds brought tidings of the same;
How that in Bethlehem was born the Son of God
    by name.
O tidings of comfort and joy, comfort and joy;
O tidings of comfort and joy.

"Fear not, then," said the angel, "Let nothing you afright,
This day is born a Savior of a pure virgin bright,
To free all those who trust in Him from Satan's
    power and might."
O tidings of comfort and joy, comfort and joy;
O tidings of comfort and joy.

The shepherds at those tidings rejoiced much in mind,
And left their flocks a-feeding in tempest, storm
    and wind,
And went to Bethl'm straightaway this blessed Babe
    to find.
O tidings of comfort and joy, comfort and joy;
O tidings of comfort and joy

But when to Bethlehem they came where our dear
    Savior lay,
They found Him in a manger where oxen feed on hay;

His mother Mary kneeling unto the Lord did pray.

O tidings of comfort and joy, comfort and joy;

O tidings of comfort and joy.

Now to the Lord sing praises, all you within this place,

And with true love and brotherhood each other now
    embrace;

This holy tide of Christmas all others doth deface.

O tidings of comfort and joy, comfort and joy;

O tidings of comfort and joy.

Feed the One You Love!

These melt-away cookies will melt in your mouth! Make them for your family, friends, and even coworkers. They won't be disappointed!

Almond Melt-Away Cookies

Cookies

       2 cups all-purpose flour

       ½ tsp. baking powder

       ¼ tsp. salt

       1 cup (2 sticks) unsalted butter, room temperature

       ¾ cup granulated sugar

       1 large egg

       2 tsp. almond extract

Icing

       1 cup powdered sugar

       1 Tbsp. milk

       1½ tsp. almond extract

Preheat the oven to 375 degrees. Line a baking sheet with parchment paper or a silicone baking mat; set aside. In a medium bowl, whisk together flour, baking powder, and salt; set aside. Using a stand mixer, beat butter and sugar until light and fluffy. Add egg and almond extract, mixing until combined. Add flour mixture ½ cup at a time, mixing until completely combined. Roll 1 tablespoon of dough into small circles and then press with hands (or with the bottom of a cup) into a disk shape. Place on the prepared baking sheet. Bake for 8 minutes. The cookies will not appear cooked, but they are. Remove from the oven and let the cookies rest on the baking sheet for 5 minutes. Then transfer to a wire rack to cool completely.

Icing

Whisk together powdered sugar, milk, and almond extract in a small bowl until smooth. Using a spoon, smooth icing onto the top of each cookie and let set for 10 minutes, or until hardened.

Makes 32 cookies

December 9

The Sweetness of the Faith

He committed no sin, nor did he ever speak in ways meant to deceive.
1 PETER 2:22

IN 1670, A CHURCH MUSIC DIRECTOR IN Cologne, Germany, faced a problem that seems very modern. After completing their part of the Christmas program, the children in his choir often grew noisy. They whispered and fidgeted. While many of his contemporaries opted to employ the switch to keep the kids under control, this choirmaster took a much sweeter approach. Visiting a local candy shop, he found some white sticks. The choirmaster had those long sweet sticks bent into the shape of a cane and purchased one for each child in his choir.

Before the long Christmas worship service, he distributed the treats and explained to the children the white color of the candy represented the purity of Christ and reflected His sinless life. The crook was to remind them of the shepherds that left their flock to pay tribute to the baby Jesus. He asked the children to consider what these candy staffs represented as they sang that day. He also gave them permission to quietly suck on the treats during the service. Legend tells us the lesson was taken to heart, and as an added bonus, the children were much better behaved during the holiday service.

Candy canes, as the bent sticks were soon called, quickly went from the choir loft to the Christmas tree. For the next two and a half centuries, they were used as one of the main decorations on evergreens all over Europe and America. In the 1920s, Bob McCormick of Albany, Georgia, found a way to hand twist colors into the candy canes. Soon several companies were using a variety of colors and patterns in their stripes, and the sticks grew even more popular. A decade later an Indiana candy maker, as a way of honoring the faith and service of his brother who was a priest, put the finishing touches on the holiday tradition. He used three stripes to symbolize the Trinity. Each stripe was red so people would recall the blood that was shed by Christ. The cane's white was retained and represented the purity of Christ, but this time the hook was formed to look like the letter *J*, standing for Jesus. For several years the man's canes were shipped with a piece of paper explaining this meaning.

In an era where so many complain about Christ being taken out of Christmas, the candy cane offers each of us a way to put Jesus back. While distributing this inexpensive sweet treat, we can tell the story of how it became a part of our holiday tradition and explain the symbolism found in its shape, colors, and stripes. The candy cane allows us the opportunity to fill the role of unthreatening missionaries and share a gentle message of hope, faith, love, joy, and salvation. Don't be surprised if your story is received as sweetly as the candy gift.

What Child Is This

The simple but touching words of "What Child Is This" is coupled with one of the most treasured and beloved English melodies of all time. "Greensleeves" dates back to the 1500s and was even employed by William Shakespeare in his play *The Merry Wives of Windsor*. Though more than twenty different lyrics have charted while using this tune, it is William Dix's words saluting a "peasant king" born in a manger that have made the deepest impression in England.

What child is this who, laid to rest,
on Mary's lap is sleeping?
Whom angels greet with anthems sweet,
while shepherds watch are keeping?
This, this is Christ the King,
whom shepherds guard and angels sing;
Haste, haste to bring him laud,
the babe, the son of Mary.

Why lies He in such mean estate,
where ox and ass are feeding?
Good Christians, fear, for sinners here
the silent Word is pleading.
This, this is Christ the King,

whom shepherds guard and angels sing;
Haste, haste to bring him laud,
the babe, the son of Mary.

So bring him incense, gold, and myrrh,
come, peasant, king, to own him;
The King of kings salvation brings,
let loving hearts enthrone him.
This, this is Christ the King,
whom shepherds guard and angels sing;
Haste, haste to bring Him laud,
the babe, the son of Mary.

Pamper the One You Love!

What's a girl to do with the winter months upon her? This body butter is a perfect solution for dry skin anywhere on your own body, or give it as a gift!

Whipped White Chocolate Body Butter

¼ cup shea butter

¼ cup cocoa butter

¼ cup coconut oil

¼ cup sweet almond oil

10-20 drops of essential oil (your choice of scent)

1 8-oz. glass jar

Combine all ingredients, except the essential oil, in a small pot or double boiler. Gently melt and stir over medium-low heat until the mixture is liquid. Remove from the heat and allow the mixture to partially set. Once partially set, add the essential oil of your choice to the mixture and whip with a hand mixer or stand mixer until the body butter is fluffy, stiff peaks have formed, and it holds its shape. Spoon the finished body butter into a cute little jar.

December 10

The Least of These

"'I was hungry and you gave me food. …I was thirsty and you gave me a drink. I was a stranger and you welcomed me. I was naked and you gave me clothes to wear. I was sick and you took care of me. I was in prison and you visited me.' Then those who are righteous will reply to him, 'Lord, when did we see you hungry and feed you, or thirsty and give you a drink? When did we see you as a stranger and welcome you, or naked and give you clothes to wear? When did we see you sick or in prison and visit you?' Then the king will reply to them, 'I assure you that when you have done it for one of the least of these brothers and sisters of mine, you have done it for me.'"

MATTHEW 25:35-40

THERE WAS A TIME IN THE NOT-SO-DISTANT past when a Christmas catalog was a child's favorite book. Corners of pages were turned down, the best choices were marked and shown to parents and friends, and millions of childhood dreams were stoked by things found in the thick annual book. Yet, as grown-ups it often seems much more difficult to choose what we want for the holidays.

In 1992, Amy Grant recorded a song that reflects Christmas from an adult point of view. With its soaring music coupled to hopeful wishes, "Grown-Up Christmas List" yearns for a time of honesty,

peace, and understanding while dreaming of a world where love never ends. While the song voices these lofty goals in simple but poetic ideals, it doesn't provide a road map for getting there.

Almost forty years before Grant recorded "Grown-Up Christmas List," a depressed actress wrote a song that has become another holiday standard. Yet, in ways that echoed the words of Jesus, Jill Jackson spelled out the formula for achieving peace on earth, goodwill to men. As it says in "Let There Be Peace On Earth," peace begins with me.

In Matthew 25:35-40, Jesus offered His disciples insight into what it took to be one of His devoted followers. To display true Christian love, they were to help the poor, hungry, imprisoned, and sick. So it's not Santa's job to deliver the most needed and important gifts; that responsibility clearly falls on us. We are to distribute the peace, honesty, love, and understanding to those in need, and if we are to do that, it means creating a new holiday list that includes more than just family and friends.

Someone you know is hurting right now. Someone you know is lonely right now. That person might need nothing more than a loving word or very simple essentials like food and clothing. Perhaps he or she just needs to realize that someone cares enough to visit. Those suffering in the darkness during this season of light should be on your Christmas list.

The way to gain peace in your world and show love to those hurting around you is to take responsibility and mirror the actions of the One whose birth we celebrate at Christmas. That means more than quoting scripture or saying prayers; it also means touching and influencing the lives of those Jesus called "the least of these." If you touch just one lost soul, then peace really can begin with you this year.

Sweet Little Jesus Boy

Negro spirituals were written mostly by field workers who had little or no education, yet in their words these slaves touched upon deep concepts often missed by the greatest preachers of that day. The unknown and enslaved person who penned "Sweet Little Jesus Boy" saw Christ as a person whose value was all but ignored. In that way the child in the manger who grew into the man that died on the cross mirrored the slave's plight. Only when we step into the writer's shoes can we fully become immersed in the message found in "Sweet Little Jesus Boy."

Sweet little Jesus Boy
They made You be born in a manguh [manger]
Sweet little Holy chil'
Didn't know who You wus [was]
Didn't know You'd come to save us Lawd
To take our sins away

Our eyes wus bline [was blind]
We couldn't see
We didn't know who You wus [was]
Long time ago You wus bawn [was born]
Bawn in a manguh [manger] low

Sweet little Jesus Boy
De worl' [the world] treat You mean, Lawd
Treat me mean too
But please, Suh, fuhgive [Sir, forgive] us Lawd
We didn't know 'twas You

Sweet little Jesus Boy
Bawn [born] long time ago
Sweet little Holy chil'
An' we didn't know who You wus [was]

Feed the One You Love!

These incredibly soft and chewy cookies have a very prominent eggnog flavor, which makes them really festive for the holiday season.

Eggnog Snickerdoodles

Cookies

> 1 cup all-purpose flour
>
> ¾ tsp. cornstarch
>
> ¾ tsp. baking powder
>
> ½ tsp. ground cinnamon
>
> ¼ tsp. ground nutmeg
>
> ⅛ tsp. salt
>
> 2 Tbsp. unsalted butter, melted
>
> ¼ cup light eggnog, room temperature
>
> 1 tsp. vanilla extract
>
> ¼ cup granulated sugar
>
> ¼ cup light brown sugar

Coating

> 3 Tbsp. granulated sugar
>
> ¼ tsp. ground cinnamon
>
> ⅛ tsp. ground nutmeg

Preheat the oven to 350 degrees. Line a baking sheet with parchment paper or a silicone baking mat; set aside. To prepare the cookies, whisk together the flour, cornstarch, baking powder, cinnamon, nutmeg, and salt in a medium bowl. In a separate large bowl, beat together the butter, eggnog, and vanilla. Stir in the granulated and brown sugars. Add in the flour mixture, stirring until just incorporated. Cover the cookie dough with plastic wrap and chill for at least 30 minutes or up to 3 hours. To prepare the coating, stir together the sugar, cinnamon, and nutmeg in a small bowl. Using a spoon, spatula, or cookie scoop, drop one portion of cookie dough into rounded mounds in the bowl of spiced sugar. Rotate it until it's fully coated; then roll it between your palms into a ball. Coat it again with the spiced sugar and place it on the prepared baking sheet. If the cookie dough was chilled longer than 1 hour, flatten the cookie dough balls slightly. Bake the cookies for 9-12 minutes. Cool on the baking sheet for 10 minutes before placing on a wire rack.

Makes 12 cookies

December 11

Tying Christmas to Easter

We have been ransomed through his Son's blood, and we have
forgiveness for our failures based on his overflowing grace, which he
poured over us with wisdom and understanding.

EPHESIANS 1:7-8

A THOUSAND YEARS AGO, THE COLORS USED at Christmas had deep meanings, and the Christians of that era treasured what those colors represented. Maybe by focusing once again on the colors of Christmas, we can fully immerse ourselves in the reason for the season, and that deals much more with Easter than with Christmas.

Martin Luther lit a candle each Christmas to remind his children that when Jesus was born there was finally a light in the darkness. It was Christ who was that light, and for early Christians, the color yellow was used to signify the hope Jesus brought to the world.

Blue had long been the color of love. Thus at many church pageants Mary was outfitted in blue because early Christians saw God's love for humankind in much the same way as a mother's deep love for her child. So someone wrapped in blue was surrounded by pure love.

Purple was the color of royalty. The fact that Jesus was the Son of God made Him the King who reigned over all other kings.

White was for purity. White was therefore a very important part of early Christmas celebrations as it symbolized the sinless nature of Christ.

The two major colors still used during Christmas were not chosen randomly. The colors that have come to be most representative of modern holidays were also the most important color symbols employed by the early church for not just the beginning of Jesus life on earth but also the end.

The red at Christmas represents the blood that was shed on the cross. That blood proved God's love for us. But it was the color that followed red that came to mean the most to those early Christians. The evergreen tree didn't slumber in the winter. It could survive the hardest and darkest days and thrive. Thus, green came to stand for the eternal life of Christ and all who followed Him. This color represents that Jesus did not die on the cross but He lives!

Christmas literally means "Christ's mass"—worship Christ. Yet what would Christmas be without Easter? Through His life and ministry Jesus taught us how to live, but it was His resurrection that provided us with the path to eternal life. So the only reason Christmas is important now is because of what happened at Easter.

This holiday season study the colors of Christ and reflect on what they symbolize. Share their meaning with others as a way of emphasizing the spiritual nature of this season. Then allow those colors to move you to a moment beyond the birth of Christ and to the real beginnings of grace: His resurrection. By focusing on the meaning of Easter, your Christmas will become much more important!

Angels We Have Heard on High

Though rarely sung until the early 1800s, some of this song's lyrics go back almost to the time of Christ. In AD 130, two centuries before Christians formally celebrated Christmas, Pope Telesphorus issued an edict that after a priest read the second chapter of Luke, the congregation should answer by singing "Gloria in excelsis Deo." So when you sing the chorus of this song, you are participating in tradition that dates back nineteen centuries.

Angels we have heard on high
sweetly singing o'er the plains,
And the mountains in reply,
echoing their joyous strains.
Gloria, in excelsis Deo!
Gloria, in excelsis Deo!

Shepherds, why this jubilee?
Why your joyous strains prolong?
What the gladsome tidings be
which inspire your heavenly song?
Gloria, in excelsis Deo!
Gloria, in excelsis Deo!

Come to Bethlehem, and see
Christ whose birth the angels sing;
Come, adore on bended knee,
Christ the Lord, the newborn King.
Gloria, in excelsis Deo!
Gloria, in excelsis Deo!

See him in a manger laid,
whom the choirs of angels praise;
Mary, Joseph, lend your aid,
while our hearts in love we raise.
Gloria, in excelsis Deo!
Gloria, in excelsis Deo!

Pamper the One You Love!

Adorable birdseed ornaments are an inexpensive activity the whole family can enjoy making during this festive holiday season. And as an added bonus, the birdseed ornaments make great gifts for family and teachers.

Birdseed Christmas Ornaments

¾ cup flour

½ cup water

3 Tbsp. corn syrup

1 envelope unflavored gelatin

4 cups birdseed

cookie cutters

parchment paper

cookie sheet

cooking spray

spoon

2 drinking straws

twine

gift tag (optional)

In a large bowl, mix together the flour, water, corn syrup, and gelatin to form a smooth paste. Slowly add the birdseed to the paste and combine until the birdseed is fully coated. Place the cookie cutters on a parchment paper–lined pan, and coat the cookie cutters with cooking spray. Spoon the birdseed mixture into the cookie cutters. Press the mixture down firmly with the back of the spoon to pack it into the cookie cutters as tightly as possible. Cut the straws into 3-inch segments, and press the straw into the top one-fourth of the birdseed-filled cookie cutter. Make sure the hole goes all the way through the mixture. Leave the straw in the ornament and allow the ornament to dry for 3-4 hours. Once the birdseed ornaments have dried, remove the straw and carefully separate the ornaments from the cookie cutters. Allow them to harden overnight. Once the ornaments are fully dry, thread a piece of twine through the hole at the top. If you are giving the ornament as a gift, add a gift tag to the piece of twine for the recipient or gift wrap carefully.

December 12

A Burning Fire

"In the same way, let your light shine before people, so they can see the good things you do and praise your Father who is in heaven."

MATTHEW 5:16

ONE OF THE ANCIENT HOLIDAY CUSTOMS IS THE burning of the Yule log. The tradition has been a part of Christmas for more than a thousand years. Even if most people don't continue the practice today, it still might be good for Christians to embrace the Yule symbolism. To do so doesn't require a fireplace but rather the warmth of a caring spirit.

Originally the Yule log burned for the entire twelve days of Christmas. For a full year the huge piece of wood was cured and rubbed with spices. On Christmas Eve the log was brought into the home. When the local church bells sounded, announcing the birth of the Savior, the woman of the house retrieved a small piece of last year's log. After washing her hands as an act of purification, a prayer was said, and three glasses of wine were poured over the new Yule log. This action represented the Trinity. After another prayer the woman lit the remaining piece of last year's log with a candle and used the old wood to light the new fire.

Thanks to having been rubbed with spices, a Yule log filled the home with a wonderful aroma when burned. That smell symbolized the gifts of the magi and the sweetness of the life of Christ. As the fire grew, the head of the home told the original Christmas story and explained the flames embodied the light that came into the world with the birth of Jesus. He then added that the larger the flames the more of person's sinful nature was consumed. It was then time for each member of the family to confess, repent, and rededicate his or her life to Christ. To visitors the Yule log was a visible sign that those who lived in this place served God and embraced the way of a Christian life.

How is the best way to ensure a Yule-log type atmosphere in your home? It begins with a welcoming spirit. Those who come to your door need to be greeted as Christ would greet them. No matter who they are, they must feel loved and accepted. Once inside your door, they also need to see visible signs of your faith. This could include a Bible open to the second chapter of Luke, a nativity scene, or a lighted candle. In other words, even if you don't quote scripture or sing an old carol, through your actions and lifestyle your visitors will be able to view your faith just as clearly as it was noted by visitors who knocked on the doors of families burning Yule logs.

The warmth of your home is the warmth others will first see in you. Your faith is the light that illuminates your home. So while you might not burn a Yule log this year, you can still be one! Shine for Christ, and let others see Him in you.

Away in a Manger

About a hundred and fifty years ago, the poem at the heart of "Away in a Manger" was matched to a tune called "Luther's Cradle Hymn." When published this musical marriage gave many the mistaken impression that Martin Luther had also penned the verses. Yet if you just read this famous carol's words, you can easily decipher its roots. Penned by an unknown American farmer almost two centuries ago, it captures the birth of Jesus from a distinctly rural point of view. Perhaps its simplicity is why it is almost as well known in children's circles as "Jesus Loves Me."

Away in a manger, no crib for a bed,
the little Lord Jesus laid down his sweet head.
The stars in the sky looked down where he lay,
the little Lord Jesus, asleep on the hay.
The cattle are lowing, the baby awakes,
but little Lord Jesus, no crying he makes.
I love thee, Lord Jesus, look down from the sky
and stay by my cradle till morning is nigh.
Be near me, Lord Jesus, I ask thee to stay
close by me forever, and love me, I pray;
Bless all the dear children in thy tender care,
and fit us for heaven to live with thee there.

Feed the One You Love!

With such a busy holiday season, why not make a treat that doesn't involve the oven? These no-bake truffles make the best gifts during the holidays. And once you dip them in white chocolate, your loved ones will keep coming back for more.

Sugar Cookie Truffles

12 sugar cookies (about 2 inches in diameter)
2 Tbsp. cream cheese, room temperature
2 cups white chocolate for melting
sprinkles for decoration

Line a baking sheet with parchment paper or a silicone mat; set aside. Place sugar cookies in a food processor and process them until they turn into fine crumbs. Add the cream cheese and process again until the mixture is well-combined and can be pressed into a ball (1-2 minutes). Shape the cookie mixture into 1- to 1½-inch balls. Place them on the baking sheet and place it in the freezer for 15 minutes or the refrigerator for 1 hour. In a medium bowl, melt the white chocolate according to the instructions on the package. Remove the cookie balls from the refrigerator. Using a spoon or two forks, dip and roll the chilled cookie balls, one at a time, in the white chocolate coating. Return them to the lined baking sheet and immediately decorate the tops with sprinkles. Repeat the process for the remaining cookie balls. Store covered in refrigerator.

Makes 18 truffles

December 13

The Power of the Written Word

First of all, I thank my God through Jesus Christ for all of you,
because the news about your faithfulness is being spread throughout
the whole world. I serve God in my spirit by preaching the good news
about God's Son, and God is my witness that I continually mention
you in all my prayers. I'm always asking that somehow, by God's
will, I might succeed in visiting you at last.

ROMANS 1:8-9

IN HIS WORDS, PAUL SHARED HIS HEART, soul, and wisdom to churches across the growing Christian world, and those words have influenced countless generations of people. Most of us can quote many of Paul's writings; we cling to their meaning and share them with others. Yet there is something else in those verses that is often overlooked and even dismissed. Paul almost always began his correspondence with gratitude. Through the opening words of his communications, those to whom he wrote felt his appreciation for their friendship. Paul's letters are therefore some of the oldest "thank-you notes" on record.

In an era where it is easy and cheap to call almost anyone, when e-mail and texting offer instant ways of written communication, and when Facebook allows everyone to see our day-to-day lives in almost minute detail, many have opted to send e-versions of Christmas cards. After all, this type of communication takes little effort and time. But perhaps the fact that e-cards are so easy and so impersonal means they make little impression on both the sender and receiver.

A Christian life should make an impact. So should a Christian greeting. It should not be hollow, lame, or easy. When someone receives a card from a person of faith, he or she should feel love and thankfulness. It should be something that moves them!

So this might just be the year to bring Christmas cards back but with a twist inspired by Paul. Make a list of your loved ones and close friends. Think about each of those people and what they have meant to your life. Dig through your relationships and find a reason not just to offer holiday greetings and the news of the past year but also to seize the chance to make an impact by thanking each person individually for something he or she has taught, given, or shared with you. Imagine the smiles and perhaps sentimental tears your sincere words will create. Perhaps for the first time some will realize that something they did has changed you and therefore changed the world. No doubt some will feel the same exhilaration of those who Paul thanked for supporting him.

It has often been said that actions speak louder than words, but when actions are combined with words, they touch people in ways that can't be measured. You have the power this Christmas to do that, but to give the gift of appreciation will take a bit of thought, time, and effort. Yet isn't that what those on your Christmas card list have already given you? Maybe it is time to thank them!

Good Christian Friends, Rejoice

Written in the Dark Ages by Heinrich Suso, this was one of the first hymns to suggest openly that living a Christian life was a reason for celebration. Ironically, many church leaders considered Suso's joyful theology so alarming he was exiled and tortured. Yet, long after those who rebuked him have been forgotten, the happiness and hope found in Suso's preaching is still resonating today in his song "Good Christian Friends, Rejoice."

Good Christian friends, rejoice
with heart and soul and voice;
give ye heed to what we say:
News, News!
Jesus Christ is born today!
Ox and ass before him bow,
and he is in the manger now.
Christ is born today,
Christ is born today!

Good Christian friends, rejoice
with heart and soul and voice;
now ye hear of endless bliss:
News, News!

Jesus Christ was born for this!
He hath opened heaven's door,
and ye are blest forevermore
Christ was born for this,
Christ was born for this!

Good Christian friends, rejoice
with heart and soul and voice;
now ye need not fear the grave:
News, News!
Jesus Christ was born to save!
Calls you one and calls you all
to gain his everlasting hall
Christ was born to save,
Christ was born to save!

Pamper the One You Love!

Having trouble finding that perfect gift for the picky family member? Why not make these easy infused olive oils, which are yummy and healthy?

Infused Olive Oils

Lemon-Infused Olive Oil

> 2 whole lemons
> ½ cup virgin olive oil
> 1 4-oz glass bottle with cork

Using a vegetable peeler, carefully strip one lemon of its zest, trying to keep each strip long and wide. If possible, avoid getting any of the white pith underneath. Place zest strips into the bottle; set aside. Zest the second lemon and set aside. In a small saucepan, heat the oil until a few small bubbles start to form. Place the zest from the second lemon into the warm oil. Let it steep for about 30 minutes. Carefully pour the lemony oil into the bottle over the uncooked strips of lemon zest, making sure to not get any of the cooked lemon zest in. Cork the bottle and store in the refrigerator. Serve drizzled over salads or in everyday cooking. Use or discard within 10-14 days.

Rosemary-Infused Olive Oil

> 3 sprigs rosemary
> ½ cup virgin olive oil
> 1 4-oz glass bottle with cork

Stuff the rosemary sprigs into the glass bottle; set aside. In a small saucepan, heat the oil until a few small bubbles start to form. Carefully pour warm oil into the bottle over the rosemary. Cork the bottle and store in the refrigerator. Serve with bread, drizzled over salads, or in everyday cooking. Use or discard within 10-14 days.

Chili-Infused Olive Oil

> 1 Tbsp. red pepper flakes
> 1-2 whole, dried Thai chilies
> ½ cup virgin olive oil
> 1 4-oz glass bottle with cork

Pour pepper flakes into the glass bottle; set aside. In a small saucepan, heat the oil until a few small bubbles start to form. Carefully pour the warm oil into the bottle over the pepper flakes. Cork the bottle and store it in the refrigerator. Serve with bread, drizzled over salads, or in everyday cooking. Use or discard within 10-14 days.

Garlic-Infused Olive Oil

½ cup whole, peeled garlic cloves

¼ cup lime juice

½ cup virgin olive oil (estimated) for baking cloves

½ cup virgin olive oil for glass bottle

1-2 4-oz glass bottles with cork

Place the garlic cloves in a bowl with the lime juice. Stir and let sit for 15 minutes. Preheat the oven to 325 degrees. Drain the lime juice from the cloves (reserving the juice for later). Spread out the garlic cloves in one layer in a small baking dish. Pour enough oil over the garlic that the cloves are completely immersed. Roast the garlic in a hot oven for 30-45 minutes. Remove from the oven and allow the garlic to cool. Remove the cloves from the oil using a slotted spoon (discard the cloves, or you can keep them to use as a paste for bread). Pour the contents into a small bowl, adding the reserved lime juice and the ½ cup olive oil for the container. Stir to combine. Carefully pour the oil into the bottle. Serve with bread, drizzled over salads, or in everyday cooking. Use or discard within 10-14 days.

Tip: If your oil starts to smoke, remove from the stove top and allow it to cool for 10 minutes.

Tip: If you plan to give the oil as a gift, decorate the bottle with ribbon or washi tape.

December 14

If You're Happy, Then Show It

"I have said these things to you so that my joy will be in you and your joy will be complete."

JOHN 15:11

IT WAS THE LATE SEVENTEENTH CENTURY, on a bright English Sunday morning that Isaac Watts Sr. preached before a polite audience at Southampton's Above Bar Congregational Church. Afterwards, as his family gathered for the noon meal, the last thing the pastor expected was his teenage son to become a critic. Yet, just as the family began to eat, Isaac Watts Jr. declared that Christian music was boring. The youth adamantly stated he was tired of singing from the Book of Psalms each Sabbath and was ready for a change. Rather than chastise his son, the elder Watts said, "Let's see you do better." The challenge was accepted, and through original hymns the younger Watts changed church music forever.

By 1719, Watts had written hundreds of personal, uplifting hymns that were being sung all over the globe. It could be said that he created the first contemporary Christmas music movement. Much of his

inspiration came directly from scripture. So it is hardly surprising that after he read Psalm 98, he was so overcome with great happiness that he penned his most famous hymn—"Joy To The World."

Even as a teen, Watts realized that Christians needed to get involved to be fully immersed in exultation. He recognized that Christianity was not a spectator sport. Hence he was willing to get to know his congregations and change services to involve members in real worship and praise. My grandmother was much the same. Though old traditions were important to her, with each passing year she found new ways to keep Christmas fresh. What Isaac Watts did for the church, Grandma did for our family. In both cases it didn't just happen, it took inspiration, planning, work, and getting to know the interests of each new member of the family. It also took one other important element.

Watts and my grandmother were both fascinated by the wonder and joy of Christmas. They loved every facet of the holidays, and they demonstrated it not only through their efforts but through their attitudes. And without a positive outlook, there is no real joy to the world.

As children most of us learned the song "If You're Happy and You Know It." This little number demanded we get involved. We clapped our hands, stomped our feet, and shouted a few times too. Largely because of the energy and enthusiasm required, "If You're Happy and You Know It" created more smiles and laughter than any church song I can remember. During this number the faces of those performing and watching lit up like Christmas trees.

This year don't go to all the effort of decorating, buying gifts, and preparing a meal without thinking of your "audience" and what they need and want. Also, don't open your door to guests without mixing in the most important element of the season—joy! Let everyone know you are happy by your actions, words, and enthusiasm, and they will want to be a part of your holiday.

Joy to the World

"Joy to the World" was inspired not by scripture from one of the four Gospels but rather from Psalm 98. So the writings of David became the anchor for Isaac Watts's most famous carol. While we sing "Joy to the World" thinking of Jesus, if we read the lyrics, we can sense the Old Testament elements employed in the compositions.

Joy to the world, the Lord is come!
let earth receive her King;
Let every heart prepare him room,
and heaven and nature sing,
and heaven and nature sing,
and heaven, and heaven, and nature sing.

Joy to the world, the Savior reigns!
Let all their songs employ;
While fields and floods, rocks, hills, and plains
repeat the sounding joy,
repeat the sounding joy,
repeat, repeat the sounding joy.

No more let sins and sorrows grow,
nor thorns infest the ground;

He comes to make his blessings flow
far as the curse is found,
far as the curse is found,
far as, far as the curse is found.

He rules the world with truth and grace,
and makes the nations prove
The glories of his righteousness
and wonders of his love,
and wonders of his love,
and wonders, wonders of his love.

Feed the One You Love!

Sfratti are traditional Italian cookies made from a spiced honey walnut filling and wrapped in flaky pie crust. They might be easy to make, but they look like you spent hours making them.

Honey Walnut Cookie Sticks (Sfratti)

> 3 frozen pie crusts, thawed
> 12 oz. finely chopped walnuts
> 2 tsp. orange zest
> ¾ tsp. ground cinnamon
> ¼ tsp. ground cloves
> 12 oz. honey
> ¾ to 1 cup all-purpose flour
> 1 egg for egg wash

Thaw the frozen pie crusts. On a lightly floured surface, roll them out into 12-inch circles. You will need three 12-inch circles. Transfer the circles to large baking sheets or large platters/plates and chill in the refrigerator until ready to use. Preheat the oven to 350 degrees. Line a baking sheet with parchment paper or a silicone baking mat; set aside.

In a medium bowl, toss together the nuts, orange zest, cinnamon, and cloves; set aside. In a medium saucepan over medium-low heat, bring the honey to a boil. Be careful, as it will foam up. When the honey starts foaming, set a timer for 5 minutes and allow it to cook while stirring constantly with a wooden spoon or silicone spatula. When the 5 minutes are up, add the nut and spice mixture, set the timer for another 5 minutes, and stir constantly. It probably won't take 5 minutes to cook, but you will know the honey/nut mixture is done when the honey no longer liquefies onto the bottom of the saucepan when you make a line through the mixture with your wooden spoon. Remove from the heat and let the mixture stand, stirring occasionally until it is cool enough to handle but not set.

While the mixture is cooling, spread the flour into a large rectangle on a piece of parchment or wax paper. Using two spoons, divide the mixture into six roughly shaped sticks approximately 6 inches long on the flour. Allow the logs to cool a bit so you are able to touch them with your fingers. Smooth out the edges so the logs aren't jagged or uneven. Remove the prepared circles from the refrigerator. Working with one dough circle at a time, cut the circle in half with a knife. Working with one stick and one half of each crust at a time, place the formed nut stick on the short/curved edge of the crust. Roll the nut stick up in the crust until you reach the long/straight edge of the crust. Cut off the excess crust on the edges of the roll, leaving about ½ inch to ¾ inch to seal the roll. Fold the trimmed edge over each side of the log and press the bottoms and sides closed firmly with your fingers. Repeat with rest of the filling logs and crust.

Place each finished stick on the baking sheet. Brush the egg wash over the top of each stick. Bake until golden, about 30 minutes. Transfer to a wire rack to cool completely. Cut into slices before serving.

Makes 48 cookie slices

December 15

Amazing and Lasting Grace

Make sure that no one misses out on God's grace. Make sure that no root of bitterness grows up that might cause trouble and pollute many people.

HEBREWS 12:15

IN 1843 WHEN CHARLES DICKENS wrote *A Christmas Carol in Prose, Being a Ghost-Story of Christmas*, now known as *A Christmas Carol*, his main objective was to expose the wretched conditions created by England's child labor and massive poverty. Dickens only chose to voice his views of this social injustice in a Christmas novel because he felt a newspaper or magazine feature would be ignored. In other words, he needed a commercial vehicle to reach his audience.

The indifference and cynicism Dickens observed on a daily basis framed his story. To the author it seemed that not even the church of that period felt much more than contempt for the poorest of the poor. So he employed a touch of humor and a scary story to drive home the need to reach out to the hopeless. Surprisingly, many understood his message, and the plight of millions was changed because of it.

What Dickens observed in his England is still with us today. There is still contempt for those Jesus called "the least of these." This attitude is exhibited most commonly in mistrust and disdain. Today, we don't have to look too hard or too far to note many things that take our minds off the real reason for the season. Beyond the blatant commercialism, it often seems that charities everywhere are seeking our donations. With so many asking for so much, it becomes easy to become like Scrooge. So how do we escape the bah-humbug trap? How do we keep joy in our hearts and grace in our actions? How do we replace pessimism with optimism and a frown with a smile?

First we have to consider what happened to Scrooge when he was finally forced to confront the result of his cynicism. By realizing what his negative attitude had cost him, he was transformed. Since Dickens was a religious man, he might well have used this plot device to mirror the transformation that happens when a lost soul is saved. Certainly grace entered Scrooge's life, and it completely altered his outlook. Life was no longer about what he could possess but rather what he could share. So, if you think about it, *A Christmas Carol* could well have been named *Amazing Grace*.

In the midst of a time when so many have such a great fear of being taken advantage of, it is important to take a step on faith. After being transformed (or saved) Scrooge found a family in need and brightened their holidays. It might just be the time for every Christian to become like old Ebenezer and share grace with a hopeless family.

O Little Town of Bethlehem

Throughout the Civil War, Phillip Brooks preached sermons that brought hope to a nation divided. Though just thirty years old, the pastor was so highly revered he presided over the funeral of Abraham Lincoln. The president's death took such a huge spiritual toll on Brooks that he resigned from the pulpit. On Christmas Eve, 1865, he was in Jerusalem, and on a whim, he rented a horse and traveled to Bethlehem. In the town where Jesus was born, Brooks not only rediscovered his faith but was given the inspiration that led to his writing "O Little Town of Bethlehem."

O little town of Bethlehem,
how still we see thee lie;
Above thy deep and dreamless sleep
the silent stars go by.
Yet in thy dark streets shineth
the everlasting light;
The hopes and fears of all the years
are met in thee tonight.

For Christ is born of Mary,
and gathered all above,
While mortals sleep, the angels keep

their watch of wondering love.
O morning stars together,
proclaim the holy birth,
And praises sing to God the King,
and peace to all on earth!

How silently, how silently,
the wondrous gift is given;
So God imparts to human hearts
the blessings of his heaven.
No ear may hear his coming,
but in this world of sin,
Where meek souls will receive him, still
the dear Christ enters in.

O holy Child of Bethlehem,
descend to us, we pray;
Cast out our sin and enter in,
be born to us today.
We hear the Christmas angels
the great glad tidings tell;
O come to us, abide with us,
our Lord Emmanuel!

Pamper the One You Love!

What could be better than hot chocolate on a cold winter's night? How about gingerbread hot chocolate? That's better!

And if you're looking for a gift to take to your friendly neighbor, just find a decorative bag, add twine, and write the instructions on a hang tag. You're neighbor will love you for it!

Gingerbread Homemade Hot Chocolate Mix

1 cup powdered sugar

¼ cup cornstarch

¾ cup unsweetened cocoa powder

½ cup powdered milk

½ tsp. salt

½ Tbsp. ground ginger

½ Tbsp. ground cinnamon

¼ Tbsp. ground cloves

⅛ tsp. ground nutmeg

2 pint jars

Combine all ingredients in a food processor or blender. Mix well. Store mix in bags or jars. If giving as a gift, decorate bag or jar with a gift tag with twine.

Makes two medium bags or jars

Brewing Instructions

> 2 Tbsp. Gingerbread Homemade Hot Cocoa Mix
>
> 1 cup milk
>
> mini marshmallows (optional)

Place two tablespoons of the gingerbread hot chocolate mixture for each cup of milk in a small saucepan. Bring contents to a boil, constantly stirring. Once hot, pour into your favorite mug. Add marshmallows, if desired.

December 16

The Blessings of Childlike Faith

"A youth here has five barley loaves and two fish. But what good is that for a crowd like this?"

JOHN 6:9

THE HISTORIC SANTA IS ACTUALLY BASED on two very dynamic Christians. The first is Nicholas of Myra, a fourth-century man of wealth who lost his parents at a young age. Raised by his uncle, the Bishop of Patara, he devoted his inheritance to the needy. Nicholas's trademark was leaving anonymous gifts. Does that remind you of someone? Six hundred years later, a Latvian duke went out every Christmas Eve taking food, clothing, and firewood to the poorest people in his country. The man we now remember as Good King Wenceslas was the second great influence for the fictional character Saint Nick.

On May 2, 1947, a time when flowers were blooming and America was watching an African American man play baseball in the major leagues for the very first time, 20th Century Fox released a Christmas movie that the studio promoted as a love story. In spite of the bizarre

93

timing of the holiday-themed movie and the fact that the crowds arrived in short sleeves and summer dresses, *Miracle on 34th Street* became an instant holiday classic and the first Hollywood film to put Santa in a starring role.

The film opens with characters that are largely cynical about Christmas and life. Faith seems to be in short supply, and commercialism is everywhere. Even the child in the movie has no use for Santa Claus or Christmas. In the story one man, blessed with childlike vision, changes everyone's perception of the holiday and what it means. Ultimately, *Miracle on 34th Street* encourages its audience to be like Santa and not give up on the childlike wonder found in the season.

Childlike vision is a vital part of faith. When most adults see a beach filled with starfish that will die if they aren't returned to the water, they sometimes become so overwhelmed by the magnitude of saving all of them that they do nothing. But a child usually responds by just saving one at a time. This trait is on display in perhaps the best known of all Christ's miracles.

The little boy who approached Jesus and the disciples with his small portion of fish and bread had that I'll-do-what-I-can attitude. He didn't worry about feeding the whole crowd; he just offered to give what he had in order to feed a few. Did Christ multiply the boy's food? He obviously could have, that would have been a small miracle for Him, but perhaps the boy's example encouraged others to share food they had been hiding for themselves. If this were the case, then that change in attitude might have been an even bigger miracle. But there is something greater at work here too. The child wasn't concerned whether the crowd deserved to be helped. In that way he was just like Christ; grace isn't earned, it is given.

If you give in joy and expect nothing back, you might just be surprised by the miracle that happens on your street this year. So embrace your childlike vision rather than being overwhelmed by an adult point of view. Don't give up because you can't do everything, just do what you can.

Good King Wenceslas

Many people feel you have to live a lot of years to make a lasting impact, but the man at the heart of this carol was murdered by his brother at just twenty-two. In spite of sitting on the Bohemian throne for just seven years, this duke so reflected the giving nature of Christ he became a vital part of the inspiration for Santa Claus. So even though his life was brief, few have had a greater impact on Christmas than Good King Wenceslas.

> Good King Wenceslas looked out
> on the Feast of Stephen,
> When the snow lay round about,
> deep and crisp and even.
> Brightly shown the moon that night,
> though the frost was cruel,
> When a poor man came in sight,
> gathering winter fuel.
>
> "Hither, page, and stand by me,
> if you know it telling,
> Yonder peasant, who is he?
> Where and what his dwelling?"
> "Sire, he lives a good league hence,

underneath the mountain,
Right against the forest fence,
by Saint Agnes' fountain."

"Bring me food and bring me wine,
bring me pine logs hither,
You and I will see him dine,
when we bear them thither."
Page and monarch, forth they went,
forth they went together,
Through the cold wind's wild lament
and the bitter weather.

"Sire, the night is darker now,
and the wind blows stronger,
Fails my heart, I know not how ;
I can go no longer."
"Mark my footsteps, my good page,
tread now in them boldly,
You shall find the winter's rage
freeze your blood less coldly."

In his master's steps he trod,
where the snow lay dinted;
Heat was in the very sod

which the saint had printed.
Therefore, Christian men, be sure,
wealth or rank possessing,
You who now will bless the poor
shall yourselves find blessing.

Feed the One You Love!

No fork is needed for these delicious apple pie cookies. Yes, you read that right! Apple PIE cookies! You might want to consider a large plate though.

Dutch Apple Pie Cookies

Cookies

> 1 roll refrigerated pie dough
>
> 5 small Granny Smith apples, peeled, cored, and diced
>
> ¼ cup granulated sugar
>
> 1 tsp. ground cinnamon
>
> 2 Tbsp. lemon juice
>
> 1 Tbsp. cornstarch

Streusel Topping

> 2¼ cups all-purpose flour
>
> ⅔ cup brown sugar
>
> ⅔ cup granulated sugar
>
> ⅔ cups old-fashioned oats
>
> pinch of salt
>
> ¾ cups plus 2 Tbsp. (14 Tbsp. total) butter, melted

Preheat the oven to 350 degrees. Spray the wells of a standard-sized muffin tin with nonstick cooking spray; set aside. Roll out the dough

onto a lightly floured surface. Using a small plastic cup, cut out circles about 2 inches in diameter. Roll unused dough and cut additional circles. Place the circles in the bottom of each muffin well.

Add the apples, sugar, cinnamon, lemon juice, and cornstarch to a medium saucepan. Cook on medium heat, stirring occasionally, for about 5-10 minutes until the apples have softened slightly and the juices begin to thicken. Remove from heat. Add about one table-spoon of the apple filling on top of each circle of pie dough. In a medium bowl, mix the flour, brown sugar, granulated sugar, oats, and salt. Add the melted butter and mix until well incorporated. Add a heaping tablespoon of the streusel topping to each muffin well, and gently pat it down over the apples. Bake for 17-19 minutes. Allow the cookies to cool in the muffin tin for at least 10-15 minutes before removing. Cool on a wire rack before serving.

Makes 2½ dozen

December 17

Witnessing . . . Words Optional

Rejoice out loud to God, our strength! / Shout for joy to Jacob's God!
PSALM 81:1

IN 1822, MINISTER CLEMENT CLARKE MOORE was lamenting that except for Catholics and Lutherans, most Americans ignored the day set aside to honor Christ's birth. Unless Christmas fell on a Sunday, Congress met on December 25, and stores stayed open while churches remained closed. In an attempt to bring a bit of the magic found in Eastern European Christmases to his children, Moore composed a whimsical poem called "A Visit from St. Nicholas." Though intended only to enhance his family's holiday, Moore's modest work, now called "'Twas the Night Before Christmas," was published in a newspaper and started a quiet revolution.

In 1840, another minister assigned his son to compose a song for a Massachusetts children's choir to sing at a Thanksgiving church service. James Pierpont was stuck for inspiration until he noted several teenage boys trying to impress local girls by racing their horse-drawn sleighs. In words and music, he painted this scene of happiness, joy,

and excitement and taught it to the local kids. Though it was anything but biblical in nature, upon its debut the song was greeted so enthusiastically the children sang it again for the community Christmas service. Thinking it was a new Christmas song, visitors from Boston and New York took it back to their cities and taught it to friends. Within three decades the imagery found in Pierpont's "Jingle Bells" would come to represent the ideal American Christmas.

"'Twas the Night Before Christmas" and "Jingle Bells," though never intended for anyone but a small audience, dramatically altered the American perception of Christmas. With its sleighs, snow, and merriment, "Jingle Bells" has visually influenced the way people see the ideal holiday in greeting cards, music, paintings, books, and film. The popularity of Moore's poem was a dramatic force in changing Christmas from a time of drinking and rowdy celebration into a holiday with the focus on children. That new view of Christmas made it a national holiday and led to all churches celebrating Christ's birth. While it might seem ironic that Saint Nick had a great deal to do with opening church doors on December 25, it proves the time-honored adage that God works in mysterious ways.

There is a wonderful old saying sometimes linked to Francis of Assisi: "Witness for Christ, and if necessary, use words." As was proved by the ministry of Christ, not all great spiritual acts happen within the walls of a church. Without meaning to Clement Clarke Moore and James Pierpont opened an American door to fully embracing Christmas and unintentionally led millions into holiday services.

Living a Christmas sermon begins with embracing the joy of the season. That joy should be seen in our eyes and heard in our voices. By sharing that joy, even in seemingly small ways like Moore and Pierpont, we live a sermon that might lead others to understand the real meaning of Christmas. By just trying to make the holidays better for one, we enhance them for all.

Jingle Bells

If you read the lyrics to "Jingle Bells," you might describe it as an 1840s Beach Boys song. After all, it deals with teenage boys trying to impress girls by racing through the streets of their town. It is therefore ironic that this American Thanksgiving carol was one of the first to actually connect snow to the holidays. When recorded by Benny Goodman and His Orchestra in 1941, it became the first Christmas song to rule the hit parade during World War II.

> Dashing thro' the snow
> in a one-horse open sleigh,
> O'er the fields we go,
> laughing all the way;
> Bells on bob tail ring,
> making spirits bright;
> What fun it is to ride and sing
> a sleighing song tonight!
>
> Jingle, bells! Jingle, bells!
> Jingle all the way!
> Oh! what fun it is to ride
> in a one-horse open sleigh!
> Jingle, bells! Jingle bells!

Jingle all the way!
Oh! what fun it is to ride
in a one-horse open sleigh!

A day or two ago
I thought I'd take a ride;
And soon Miss Fanny Bright
was seated by my side.
The horse was lean and lank;
misfortune seemed his lot;
He got into a drifted bank,
and we, we got upsot.

Jingle, bells! Jingle, bells!
Jingle all the way!
Oh! what fun it is to ride
in a one-horse open sleigh!
Jingle, bells! Jingle bells!
Jingle all the way!
Oh! what fun it is to ride
in a one-horse open sleigh!

Pamper the One You Love!

If you have any leftover cookies during this holiday season, why not use them to make cookie butter? Spooning the cookie butter into jars and adding a simple paper label make this homemade treat the perfect gift. Of course, you might have trouble getting it away from your family—especially if you make it from their particularly favorite cookie!

Cookie Butter

> 2 cups cookie crumbs (number of cookies will vary depending on size and shape)
>
> ½ stick butter
>
> ½ cup sweetened condensed milk
>
> ¼ cup evaporated milk

Place whole cookies into a food processor (removing any filling first—such as from an Oreo or a Nutter Butter). Blend the cookies until they form a very fine powder. In a small saucepan, heat the butter over low heat until melted, and then stir in the sweetened condensed milk and evaporated milk until melted together. Pour ½ cup of the liquid into the cookie crumbs and mix with a spoon. Keep adding small amounts of the liquid until the cookie butter is just wet enough to bond together. Once blended, allow the butter to chill in the refrigerator (estimated an hour or two) before eating. You can spread the cookie butter on toast, bagels, pancakes, or waffles or use it as a dip. Store the cookie butter in the refrigerator for up to two weeks.

Makes 1½ cups

Tip: If you are giving the cookie butter as a gift, place in a decorated Mason jar, with an applied label of its contents.

December 18

The Most Powerful Gifts

And serve each other according to the gift each person has received, as good managers of God's diverse gifts.

1 PETER 4:10

YESTERDAY THE DEVOTIONAL CENTERED on making an impact, but where and how do we live a sermon? Perhaps you can find a starting point in a song written in 1941 by a Wellesley College piano teacher.

Katherine Davis was an avid reader who was enamored with a European folktale centering on children trying to find just the right gift to share with the baby Jesus. Davis contrasted this ancient story with what she had witnessed in America during the Great Depression. With those two thoughts in mind, Davis developed lyrics based on a poor little boy who came to visit Christ in the manger and felt a desperate need to give the baby a gift.

"The Carol of the Drum" remained all but unknown for almost two decades until discovered by Harry Simeone. He renamed Davis's carol "Little Drummer Boy" and rushed his choir into the studio. In the midst of the rock-and-roll explosion, the story of a poor child and his drum took the nation by storm. It now ranks behind only "White Christmas" and "Rudolph the Red-Nosed Reindeer" in holiday sales.

As the song's lyrics spell out, the little boy is convinced he has nothing of value to give. As he views people leaving gifts for Jesus, he is left feeling inadequate and sad. "Little Drummer Boy" then shares a biblical truth—what you can purchase is not nearly as valuable as sharing the talents God has given to you. In the end it was the child playing the drum that made the greatest impact.

Even if you are hesitant about displaying them, God has graced you with talents, and you can use them to lift and inspire others. So as you look toward the last week before Christmas, reframe your thinking from *What can I buy?* to *What can I give?*

Most communities have programs that distribute toys and foods to poor families. They almost always need volunteers to package or deliver those gifts. Other groups are looking for cookies or presents for those who are in jail or the hospital. Your vision should also easily identify people in your neighborhood or church who have no family this holiday season. Perhaps you can visit them and share a bit of the Christmas spirit. And that is just the beginning. God can use your smiles and kind words to touch the souls of His forgotten people. In fact, those might be your most powerful gifts.

Here is the bottom line: Don't be shy! Don't choose to not serve, but rather find a place that needs help and make that your mission this week. As the great Christian doctor Albert Schweitzer once told a college class, "I don't know what your destiny will be, but I do know: the only ones among you who will truly be happy are those who have sought and found how to serve." So seek out a place to serve, and grab a large dose of Christmas happiness in the process!

The First Noel

There has long been a war over which country gave "The First Noel" to the world. Both England and France have claimed this carol as their own. There are even two spellings for the last word in the title. On one side of the channel, it is "Noel" while it is "Nowell" on the other. Though first published in France, the song's tune and phrasing seem to reflect the style used in rural England during the 1500s. Thus this is likely one of the few true Christmas folk songs that is still sung today.

The first Noel the angel did say
was to certain poor shepherds in fields as they lay;
in fields where they lay keeping their sheep,
on a cold winter's night that was so deep.
Noel, Noel, Noel, Noel,
born is the King of Israel.

They looked up and saw a star
shining in the east, beyond them far;
and to the earth it gave great light,
and so it continued both day and night.
Noel, Noel, Noel, Noel,
born is the King of Israel.

And by the light of that same star
three Wise Men came from country far;
to seek for a king was their intent,
and to follow the star wherever it went.
Noel, Noel, Noel, Noel,
born is the King of Israel.

This star drew nigh to the northwest,
o'er Bethlehem it took its rest;
and there it did both stop and stay,
right over the place where Jesus lay.
Noel, Noel, Noel, Noel,
born is the King of Israel.

Then entered in those Wise Men three,
full reverently upon their knee,
and offered there, in his presence,
their gold and myrrh and frankincense.
Noel, Noel, Noel, Noel,
born is the King of Israel.

Feed the One You Love!

Gingersnaps are a holiday classic and a family favorite that never disappoint. With spicy ginger, cinnamon, and sweet molasses, this recipe will keep the kiddos coming back for more!

Classic Gingersnaps

       ¾ cup shortening
       ¼ cup light molasses
       1 egg
       2 cups flour
       1 cup sugar
       2 tsp. baking soda
       1 tsp. cinnamon
       1 tsp. ginger
       extra sugar, optional

Preheat the oven to 350 degrees. Line a baking sheet with parchment paper or a silicone baking mat; set aside. In a large bowl, cream the shortening and sugar. Add the molasses and egg and beat again until everything is combined. Sift together the dry ingredients and add to the creamed mixture. Mix well. Roll in small balls (about 1 to 1½ inches in diameter). Drop in extra sugar, if desired, and roll the cookie balls until fully coated in sugar. Place 2 inches apart on the prepared cookie sheet. Bake for about 7-10 minutes. Cool on the baking sheet several minutes, then transfer to a wire rack to cool completely.

Makes 18 cookies

December 19

Becoming the Christmas Bell

*"I assure you that you will cry and lament, and the world will be
happy. You will be sorrowful, but your sorrow will turn into joy."*
JOHN 16:20

YESTERDAY WE CONSIDERED PLACES OF service. Today we need to
make it even more personal. There are more suicides during the week
leading up to Christmas than there are at any other time of the year.
It is during holidays that loneliness is most magnified. So to be like
Christ, we must think beyond our own lives and seek out those who
are drowning in sorrow.

Henry Wadsworth Longfellow is often cited as America's greatest
poet. At the start of the Civil War, Longfellow was married, had five
children, and was a professor at Harvard. It was during that time a
series of tragedies challenged the great man's faith. While lighting a
match, Longfellow's wife's clothes caught fire, and she burned to death.
Next his nineteen-year-old son, Charles, was badly wounded in battle.
The final blow that brought the literary giant to his knees was several
of his most beloved students dying in bloody battlefields. Thus, by

113

1863, the once great man of faith was lost in a suicidal cloud of despair.

On December 25th, the ringing of Christmas bells inspired Longfellow to write. The words that poured from the man's deeply troubled soul were ominous and foreboding. Longfellow spelled out in verse that God had deserted him and the world. Yet, as line after line found its way onto paper and the church bells rang louder, the poet suddenly felt the Lord in his midst. He finished what would become his best known work with these words, "God is not dead, nor doth He sleep. The wrong shall fail, the right prevail, with peace on earth, goodwill to men."

During the Civil War, "I Heard the Bells on Christmas Day" brought many who were on the brink of giving up a reason to live. Reworked into a song, the poet's words have continued to bring hope to millions during the last century and a half. So, while healing a wounded writer's soul, this carol has brought hope to a nation in its greatest times of need.

Most of us don't have the talent to write a healing poem to share with a hurting world, but we should have the desire to visit with those who feel as Longfellow felt when he began writing "I Heard the Bells on Christmas Day." What many need is the assurance that someone notices their sadness and cares enough to listen as they voice their troubles. By allowing them to put words to their pain and to have someone hear those words, these troubled souls might just come to see the light the poet found on Christmas Day 1863.

There are no magic words that will heal a broken heart and a beaten spirit, but the presence of a person emulating Christ by seeking out the lost and forgotten might be what is needed for a troubled soul to move forward. By reaching out and listening, you could be proving to the lost and forgotten that God is not dead nor does He sleep. Seek out the lonely and lost, and open your ears and arms to them.

I Heard the Bells on Christmas Day

Henry Wadsworth Longfellow is perhaps the greatest poet America has ever known. "The Song of Hiawatha," "The Courtship of Miles Standish," and "Evangeline" have been studied in depth on college campuses for more than a century and a half. Yet, thanks to an Englishman named John Calkin, who set "I Heard the Bells on Christmas Day" to music, it is this Longfellow Christmas poem that has touched more people than all of the poet's other works combined.

I heard the bells on Christmas day
Their old familiar carols play,
And wild and sweet the words repeat
Of peace on earth, goodwill to men.

I thought how, as the day had come,
The belfries of all Christendom
Had rolled along th'unbroken song
Of peace on earth, goodwill to men.

And in despair I bowed my head:
"There is no peace on earth," I said,
"For hate is strong, and mocks the song
Of peace on earth, goodwill to men!"

Then pealed the bells more loud and deep:
"God is not dead, nor doth He sleep;
The wrong shall fail, the right prevail,
With peace on earth, goodwill to men."

Then ringing, singing on its way,
The world revolved from night to day—
A voice, a chime, a chant sublime
of peace on earth, goodwill to men!

Pamper the One You Love!

Keep everyone you know warm and cozy this winter with a cute jar of chai tea mix. It has been proved that chai improves the digestive system and also enhances the immune system, fights inflammation, and has antioxidant properties.

Chai Tea Kit

> 2 Tbsp. green cardamom pods
>
> 4 whole star anise
>
> 6 3-inch cinnamon sticks
>
> 1 Tbsp. fennel seeds
>
> 2 tsp. whole cloves
>
> 2 tsp. whole black peppercorns
>
> 2 tsp. coriander seeds
>
> ½ cup chopped candied ginger
>
> 1½ cups loose black tea
>
> 17-oz. clamp jar (if given as gifts, use five 4-oz. jars)

Preheat the oven to 350 degrees. Split the cardamom pods open lengthwise with a sharp paring knife to expose the seeds. Spread out the cardamom, star anise, cinnamon, fennel, cloves, peppercorns, and coriander in an even layer on a small baking sheet. Toast the spices in the oven for 5-10 minutes. After cooling, move the toasted spices to a sealable plastic bag, and use a rolling pin to crush them into small pieces, making the contents small enough to fit inside a fillable tea bag or mesh tea ball. Use a mortar and pestle if you are having difficulty with the rolling pin. Mix together the spices, chopped ginger, and black tea in a bowl, and transfer to a jar for storage or gifting.

Makes about 2½ cups (about 40 prepared cups) of tea

Brewing Instructions

> 1-2 tablespoons chai tea mix
> 1 cup boiling water
> ¼ cup hot milk
> honey or sugar to taste

Fill a tea bag or mesh tea ball with 1-2 tablespoons of chai tea mix. Steep tea in 1 cup boiling water for about 5 minutes. Remove the tea bag and add ¼ cup hot milk, heated in the microwave or in a small saucepan. Stir in honey or sugar to taste.

Tip: If you are looking for gift ideas, package the chai tea mixture with a mesh tea ball or fillable tea bags. Don't forget to add a hang tag with the brewing directions.

December 20

Escaping Bondage

Therefore, since we have been made righteous through his
faithfulness, we have peace with God through our Lord Jesus Christ.
ROMANS 5:1

NOT LONG AFTER THE CIVIL War, John Work began to collect and publish Negro spirituals for the Fisk Jubilee Singers. One of the most stirring of these anthems was "Go Tell It on the Mountain." When we sing this uplifting carol today, we rarely pause to consider where it was birthed and what the plight of the song's writer can teach us.

Slavery has been called America's original sin. Capturing, forcibly importing, and enslaving a race of people certainly stands directly in the face of the ideals on which our nation was founded. Oppressed, uneducated, living lives without freedom, suffering incredible cruelty and humiliation and often treated as less than human, somehow many African-American slaves came to believe in the saving power of the baby born in a manger. Perhaps this message took root because the slaves had been assured that Christ died for all people. That meant Jesus respected and valued those no one else did. These saved slaves realized that in the eyes of God every soul was equal.

Though they had little chance of ever being anything but a piece of property, many slaves became such devoted Christians they were moved to impart that faith to others. The vehicle most often employed in sharing the good news was original music of unparalleled power and grace. "Go Tell It on the Mountain" was one of the songs that was born in the fields and somehow found its way into the hands of John Work.

Though this song's writer could likely not read and had no real hope of ever being free from the chains of slavery, his understanding of the birth of Jesus and the gift of salvation was much more accurate and compelling than most sermons delivered by university-educated pastors. The writer comprehended that while life might be full of troubles, pain, and disappointments there was reason to celebrate because Jesus promised eternal freedom down the road. In his simple but profound lyrics, the writer of "Go Tell It on the Mountain" not only painted the story of Christ's birth but also presented the reason Jesus had come to earth.

Most humans are slaves to something. For a select few, what binds them are things that will require professional help to escape. But for most it is worry that locks the chains of bondage. Unlike the American slave who had no path to freedom, faith should guide us away from worry. So perhaps the greatest gift you can give yourself this holiday season is to let God handle what you cannot.

In just five days, we will mark Christmas. If a slave could be so excited about the birth of Jesus he wanted to shout it from a mountaintop, then surely we can overlook the disappointments in our lives, free ourselves from worrying about things we can't change, and join in this celebration with enthusiasm and thankfulness.

Go Tell It on the Mountain

For the American slave, thoughts could easily be expressed in one way—music. Written and sung in fields, this folk music combined elements from Africa and America to create a new type of expression. Thousands of songs were written, but as most were never transcribed, only a few hundred survive. As is seen in "Go Tell It on the Mountain," the most commonly employed lyrical theme involved hope found in God's grace. Few of these writers would ever know equality on earth, but they fully understood they were equal in God's eyes. And that was something to sing about.

> Go, tell it on the mountain,
> over the hills and everywhere;
> Go, tell it on the mountain
> that Jesus Christ is born!
>
> While shepherds kept their watching
> o'er silent flocks by night,
> Behold! thro'out the heavens
> there shone a holy light.
> Go, tell it on the mountain,
> over the hills and everywhere;
> Go, tell it on the mountain
> that Jesus Christ is born!

The shepherds feared and trembled
when lo! above the earth
Rang out the angel chorus
that hailed our Savior's birth.
Go, tell it on the mountain,
over the hills and everywhere;
Go, tell it on the mountain
that Jesus Christ is born!

Down in a lowly manger
the humble Christ was born,
And brought us God's salvation
that blessed Christmas morn.
Go, tell it on the mountain,
over the hills and everywhere;
Go, tell it on the mountain
that Jesus Christ is born!

Feed the One You Love!

Yeah, you can thank me in advance. Just the word *gooey* makes you want to make them!

Gooey Butter Cookies

½ cup butter, softened

8 oz. cream cheese, softened

1 egg

¼ tsp. vanilla extract

1 box yellow butter cake mix

1 cup powdered sugar

Preheat the oven to 350 degrees. Line a baking sheet with parchment paper or a silicone baking mat; set aside. Combine the butter, cream cheese, egg, and vanilla in a medium bowl and cream using a mixer until light and fluffy. Stir in the dry cake mix until the dough becomes thick but smooth. Cover the cookie dough with plastic wrap and chill for at least 30 minutes. Pour the powdered sugar into a separate bowl; set aside. Scoop a spoonful of the cookie dough and roll into a ball, then roll the ball in the powdered sugar until fully coated. Place the cookie balls on the prepared baking sheet and bake for 12 minutes. Cool on the baking sheet for a few minutes then transfer to a wire rack to cool completely.

December 21

The Message in the Branches

"God so loved the world that he gave his only Son, so that everyone who believes in him won't perish but will have eternal life."

JOHN 3:16

AT THE HEART OF MOST PEOPLE'S Christmas decorations is a tree. Some cut them down, others buy them at special lots, and many simply unpack them from boxes. Each year millions of trees appear in homes, stores, schools, and parks as a time-honored symbol of the holidays. Depending upon the use of lighting and ornaments, trees can appear traditional or modern. Some are just inches tall and sit on tables, and others reach toward the skies in city parks. Large or small, real or artificial, the tree is essential to the holidays. This year, after your tree is in place, perhaps it's time to take a deeper look at why that evergreen is a part of the celebration of a Savior's birth and how we can use it to reflect upon God's greatest promise. Essentially, this story begins with a monk.

Boniface was an early Christian missionary. Only six hundred years after Christ walked the earth, this priest from Devonshire,

England traveled across Europe sharing the story of Jesus. On one of his trips, he came across a band of men gathered around a large oak tree, preparing to sacrifice a small boy to the god Thor. Legend has it that the alarmed missionary, in an attempt to stop the child's murder, rushed forward and struck the tree with his fist. The mighty oak fell to the ground, revealing a small fir just behind it. Having captured the men's attention, Boniface explained the evergreen tree stood for the eternal life offered by Christ, and the fir's triangular shape represented the Trinity of the Father, Son, and Holy Ghost. Not only was the child saved but the men became Christians.

Following Boniface's lead, other missionaries began using the evergreen tree as a symbol of eternal life. By 1200, many Christians embraced this symbolism to the point they brought trees into their homes at Christmas as a way of remembering the reason God came to earth in the form of a child.

As time passed more elements were added to the symbolism of the tree. Since everlasting life had been launched from a cross, the wood found in the trunk came to represent the sacrifice of Christ, and the green limbs springing from that trunk stood for the Resurrection. Martin Luther then added a candle to represent the light that came into the darkness when Christ was born. After that, red decorations were used as a way of remembering the blood Jesus shed for sins.

This year when you look at a Christmas tree, recall the manner in which early missionaries employed the evergreen to spell out the story of salvation. Study the tree's shape and reflect upon the Trinity and what it means to you. And don't allow your eyes to leave that tree until you think of the promise found in John 3:16. The green in that tree stands for everlasting life, and because of the Resurrection, Christmas will be celebrated this year, next year, and for all of eternity.

O Christmas Tree

By the Middle Ages, most people in Germany cut a tree and brought it into their homes at Christmas. During the dark days of winter, just the act of setting the evergreen in a home and smelling its sweet scent lifted spirits. Families not only offered prayers of thanksgiving while gathered around the tree, they also sang familiar carols. It wasn't long before an ancient folk song, "O Denneboom," was rewritten to describe the joy delivered by the arrival and decorating of the Christmas tree.

O Christmas Tree! O Christmas Tree!
Thy leaves are so unchanging;
O Christmas Tree! O Christmas Tree!
Thy leaves are so unchanging;
Not only green when summer's here,
But also when 'tis cold and drear.
O Christmas Tree! O Christmas Tree!
Thy leaves are so unchanging!

O Christmas Tree! O Christmas Tree!
Much pleasure thou can'st give me;
O Christmas Tree! O Christmas Tree!
Much pleasure thou can'st give me;

How often has the Christmas tree
Afforded me the greatest glee!
O Christmas Tree! O Christmas Tree!
Much pleasure thou can'st give me.

O Christmas Tree! O Christmas Tree!
Thy candles shine so brightly!
O Christmas Tree! O Christmas Tree!
Thy candles shine so brightly!
From base to summit, gay and bright,
There's only splendor for the sight.
O Christmas Tree! O Christmas Tree!
Thy candles shine so brightly!

O Christmas Tree! O Christmas Tree!
How richly God has decked thee!
O Christmas Tree! O Christmas Tree!
How richly God has decked thee!
Thou bidst us true and faithful be,
And trust in God unchangingly.
O Christmas Tree! O Christmas Tree!
How richly God has decked thee!

Pamper the One You Love!

If you are looking for that perfect mud mask, we have one to share with you. It not only makes the perfect gift, but you can store your mask mix for later use.

Lavender and Lemon Oatmeal Mud Mask

      1 cup oatmeal

      1 Tbsp. lavender petals

      2-3 drops lavender essential oil

      2-3 drops lemon essential oil

      2 capsules of vitamin E

      5 Tbsp. of Pascalite or bentonite clay

      glass storage jar

Most natural health stores carry both Pascalite and bentonite clay. These clays are unique because when they are mixed with fluid, they produce an "electrical charge" that draws out toxins and impurities from the skin. Combine oatmeal and lavender flowers in a food processor, using the chop feature to grind them to a fine powder. Add the lavender and lemon essential oils. Puncture the vitamin E capsules and squeeze the liquid into your mixture. Mix until well blended. Carefully add the clay with a wooden spoon. (The mixture will be very powdery and can cause big puffs if you drop the clay on it.) Place your mix in a jar for storage or in a Mason or clamp jar for a gift.

Instructions for Use

    Lavender and lemon oatmeal mud mask

    milk

To use, combine desired amount of the mask with enough milk to make a thin paste. You don't want it to be runny, but if it is too thick it will not spread across your face easily. This can be used as a refreshing face mask or face scrub. When finished, wash off your face with cool water.

December 22

X Marks the Spot

"The Pharisee stood and prayed about himself with these words,
'God, I thank you that I'm not like everyone else—crooks, evildoers,
adulterers—or even like this tax collector.'"

LUKE 18:11

ANGER CREATES A VACUUM THAT CAN suck all the joy out of the season. The attitude that provokes anger is similar to that of the Pharisee in today's scripture. Sadly, even though Jesus taught us to embrace everyone as an equal and love all as brothers and sisters, many can't help but judge. In almost every case, unnecessary judgment links Christians to Pharisees rather than to Jesus.

Some people get deeply upset when businesses or people spell *Christmas* as *Xmas*. In a way, this is the same kind of trap the Pharisees employed on Jesus. Christ wisely turned traps like this into great spiritual lessons. This is the year we should do the same. One of the best ways to deal with *Xmas* is to share its very Christian origins. This defuses a potential argument and provides a chance to witness.

Since the very beginning, the letter X has been linked to Christianity. X is the first letter of Christ's name in Greek, so many early Christians put an X over their doors to display that people of faith lived in that home. For centuries those who could not read used the letter X when asked to write their faith on a piece of paper or in the dirt. Everyone knew that letter signified a follower of Jesus.

The letter X's association with Christmas can be traced back to when the church first started celebrating the holiday in AD 320. For more than a thousand years many church leaders wrote *Xmas* rather than *Christmas* for a number of reasons. As most believers could not read, using an X, which was almost always associated with Christ, provided instant recognition to the saved and the lost. Also, a majority of people knew that *mas* meant worship. Therefore, when the letter and the word came together, *Xmas* meant "worship Christ."

Another reason the early church used Xmas rather than writing out Christmas was based on practicality. In many places ink and paper were expensive and rare. Cutting costs by saving materials was a common practice. Thus the X standing for Christ was often used in letters and announcements.

Though some today might employ *Xmas* as a way of trying to remove Christ from the holidays, those who know the origin of this practice have an opening to use this practice to gently share their faith. They can point out that for centuries X identified Christians, and *Xmas* actually means "worship Christ." Also, reacting to "Happy Holidays" with a "Merry Christmas" is another peaceful way of putting Christ's name into the holiday mix. The key for drawing people into understanding faith is having a Christlike attitude. This Christmas, rather than confront, gently teach.

O Come, O Come, Emmanuel

While there are elements of other Christmas songs that might pre-date "O Come, O Come, Emmanuel," this carol is likely the oldest that is still sung with original music and lyrics. Penned in Latin more than eleven centuries ago by a cleric who had a deep understanding of scripture, except for being translated into scores of languages, it has remained all but unchanged. Thus, when we sing this song, we are fully connected to countless generations who worship a Savior during Christmas.

O come, O come, Emmanuel,
and ransom captive Israel,
that mourns in lonely exile here
until the Son of God appear.
Rejoice! Rejoice! Emmanuel
shall come to thee, O Israel.

O come, thou Wisdom from on high,
and order all things far and nigh;
to us the path of knowledge show
and cause us in her ways to go.
Rejoice! Rejoice! Emmanuel
shall come to thee, O Israel.

O come, O come, great Lord of might,
who to thy tribes on Sinai's height
in ancient times once gave the law
in cloud and majesty and awe.
Rejoice! Rejoice! Emmanuel
shall come to thee, O Israel.

O come, thou Root of Jesse's tree,
an ensign of thy people be;
before thee rulers silent fall;
all peoples of thy mercy call.
Rejoice! Rejoice! Emmanuel
shall come to thee, O Israel.

O come, thou Key of David, come,
and open wide our heavenly home.
The captives from their prison free,
and conquer death's deep misery.
Rejoice! Rejoice! Emmanuel
shall come to thee, O Israel.

O come, thou Dayspring, come and cheer
our spirits by thy justice here;
disperse the gloomy clouds of night,
and death's dark shadows put to flight.

Rejoice! Rejoice! Emmanuel
shall come to thee, O Israel.

O come, Desire of nations bind
all peoples in one heart and mind.
From dust thou brought us forth to life;
deliver us from earthly strife.
Rejoice! Rejoice! Emmanuel
shall come to thee, O Israel.

Feed the One You Love!

You might not be hungry now, but when you see these tasty cookies, you'll be more than hungry. This quick and easy recipe will feed the hungriest of those you love!

Snickers Cookie Bars

Shortbread Layer

> ⅔ cup butter, softened
>
> ¼ cup sugar
>
> 1¼ cup all-purpose flour
>
> ¼ tsp. salt
>
> 1 tsp. pure vanilla extract

Caramel Layer

> 1 11-oz. bag caramels
>
> ¼ cup heavy cream
>
> 1 cup dry roasted (plain) peanuts

Chocolate Layer

> 12 oz. milk chocolate chips

Preheat the oven to 350 degrees. Line a 9 x 9-inch baking dish with parchment paper; set aside. Cream together the butter, sugar, flour, salt, and vanilla until fully incorporated and crumbly. Press the

shortbread mixture into the bottom of the lined baking dish and cook for approximately 20 minutes, until slightly golden. Remove from the oven and set aside. Place the caramels and the cream in a microwave-safe bowl and microwave for 2 minutes, stirring every 30 seconds. Stir in the peanuts, and pour the mixture evenly over the shortbread, using a spoon to distribute the caramel evenly. Allow to cool for at least 10 minutes. In a microwave-safe bowl, heat the chocolate chips in increments of 30 seconds, stirring each time, until melted. Pour the chocolate over the caramel and spread evenly. Allow the chocolate to cool and harden completely before serving, about 2 hours. Cut into squares and serve.

Makes 9-12 bars

December 23

Opening Our Eyes to Joy

"Glory to God in heaven, and on earth peace among those whom he favors."

LUKE 2:14

THERE IS A WONDERFUL AND WISE OLD SAYING, "Take time to stop and smell the roses." Perhaps we need to expand that old adage at Christmas to bring in even more of our senses. After all, Christmas is a time when everything in our world seems to change. Homes and businesses are decorated; there are colorful lights on every block; holiday events at schools; community celebrations, parades, parties, special services at almost every church; and holiday music plays from loudspeakers. During this time of the year, people seem to be more outgoing and robust, and there really is a spirit of goodwill that can be seen in almost everyone you meet. And none of this would be happening if not for the birth of a child named Jesus. Now that is something to celebrate!

During the cold winter's days of 1950, Broadway tunesmith Meredith Wilson took in the wonders of Christmas in New York. The

Iowa native noted Santas on every corner, snowflakes falling, bells ringing, and bundled-up kids spying into every frosty storefront window. Ten months later, when on vacation at the Grand Hotel in Yarmouth, Nova Scotia, Wilson took his observations of the holidays from his rural youth, combined them with those he had noted in the Big Apple the previous year, and penned "It's Beginning to Look a Lot Like Christmas."

"It's Beginning to Look a Lot Like Christmas" was initially sandwiched into a Broadway musical that closed not long after opening. This upbeat look at the holidays would have likely been lost forever if Perry Como had not been one of the few who caught the show. In 1951 the popular television host recorded Wilson's take on Christmas, and it became an instant holiday classic.

People were likely drawn to "It's Beginning to Look a Lot Like Christmas" for two reasons. Wilson created a song that happily captured the magic of the holidays. Its lyrics made people smile. The other reason for the number's immediate impact was Perry Como. The popular crooner was as upbeat, warm, and joyful as the song he took up the charts. There is a great lesson in embracing Wilson's lyrics as well as Como's style. To fully enjoy these special moments, we must first take the time to notice and embrace every facet of the holidays as well as adopt a positive, gentle, friendly attitude when dealing with others. That is a combination that should assure happiness.

Once you have considered the words to the Perry Como holiday hit and studied a world immersed in the trappings of the season, take another moment to look into the mirror. What is reflected there? When people see you will they say, "Yes, it is beginning to look at lot like Christmas," because it's written all over *your* face, or will they see someone who reflects none of the happiness of the season? If you are a Christian, if you believe that Christmas was the beginning of the greatest story ever lived, then smiling and showing joy should come easily.

Silent Night

The fact that we know this carol is a miracle. Two centuries ago, when a priest and schoolteacher hurriedly combined a three-year-old poem with new music, it was because their little Austrian church's organ wouldn't play. So "Silent Night" was only meant to be a stopgap measure used for one Christmas service. But a few weeks later, the song's writers played the carol for the man who came to fix the organ, and after writing down the words and music, this traveling music repairman took the song all across Europe, teaching it to children everywhere he worked. He was thus the Johnny Appleseed for the world's most popular carol.

Silent night, holy night,
All is calm, all is bright
Round yon virgin mother and child.
Holy infant so tender and mild,
Sleep in heavenly peace,
Sleep in heavenly peace.

Silent night, holy night,
Shepherds quake at the sight;
Glories stream from heaven afar,
Heavenly hosts sing Alleluia!

Christ, the Savior, is born,
Christ, the Savior, is born!

Silent night, holy night,
Son of God, love's pure light;
Radiant beams from thy holy face
With the dawn of redeeming grace,
Jesus, Lord, at thy birth,
Jesus, Lord, at thy birth.

Pamper the One You Love!

With the cold weather keeping you inside, why don't you use the time indoors to make some keepsake gifts for those you love? Not only are they easy to make but it only costs you a few dollars to make them!

Photo Pendant

> Diamond Glaze dimensional adhesive
> 1 1-inch pendant tray with glass
> photos printed to desired size on heavy-duty paper
>   or cardstock
> X-Acto knife
> multipurpose adhesive (clear)
> rubber mallet
> chain, ribbon, or key ring

Separate the pendant tray into pieces. Add a small amount of the Diamond Glaze to the back of the glass circle. Spread the glaze around the circle with the tip of the dispenser or a toothpick. Press the glass piece gently on top of the photo to remove bubbles. Hold for 30 seconds; allow to dry overnight. The next day, using an X-Acto knife, cut the excess paper and extra dried glaze from around the glass piece. Add a small amount of multipurpose adhesive to the inside of the pendant and press the glass piece with the photo into the pendant. If needed, tap the glass piece into the pendant using the rubber mallet. Using the X-Acto knife, remove any extra glue or paper that may have pushed out around the edges of the pendant. Allow to dry 4 hours. Place the pendant on any chain, ribbon, or key ring you choose. Wrap and give as a gift, or keep it for yourself!

December 24

Home

After Jesus was born in Bethlehem in the territory of Judea during the rule of King Herod, magi came from the east to Jerusalem. They asked, "Where is the newborn king of the Jews? We've seen his star in the east, and we've come to honor him." When King Herod heard this, he was troubled....He gathered all the chief priests and the legal experts and asked them where the Christ was to be born. They said, "In Bethlehem of Judea, for this is what the prophet wrote: You, Bethlehem, land of Judah, by no means are you least among the rulers of Judah, because from you will come one who governs, who will shepherd my people Israel." Then Herod secretly called for the magi and ...sent them to Bethlehem, saying, "Go and search carefully for the child. When you've found him, report to me so that I too may go and honor him." When they heard the king, they went; and look, the star they had seen in the east went ahead of them until it stood over the place where the child was. When they saw the star, they were filled with joy. They entered the house and saw the child with Mary his mother. Falling to their knees, they honored him. Then they opened their treasure chests and presented him with gifts of gold, frankincense, and myrrh. Because they were warned in a dream not to return to Herod, they went back to their own country by another route.

MATTHEW 2:1-12

"I'LL BE HOME FOR CHRISTMAS" contains just a dozen lines. Inspired by a man who wanted to leave college and see his girlfriend back home, then written by two others on one of the hottest days of summer, this classic holiday hit was embraced by millions during World War II as more prayer than song. Introduced by Bing Crosby on October 4, 1943, it remains one of the few secular carols to strike deep emotional chords with each new generation.

Home is a destination point during the holidays. Millions endure incredible hardships to once again reunite with families. It is so much a part of our culture it has inspired movies, books, and songs. Yet few of those caught up in getting home for Christmas stop to consider when this tradition began.

Jesus was born in Bethlehem because Mary and Joseph had to go home to be counted in a census. Thus the very first Christmas tradition was actually about going home.

Webster defines *home* as a place where someone lives. In truth, this should be the definition of a house. A home is where memories are made. A home is warm and welcoming, and it offers a refuge from trying times. Home is really where the heart is. And in all those ways, Christmas is home.

Tonight, while children are looking through windows for Santa, take the time to search your life, family, and heart to see if you can find evidence of the One who went home to Bethlehem to be born. If not, it is time to embrace the oldest Christmas tradition and ask Jesus to come home to your heart again.

O Holy Night!

In 1906, Reginald Fessenden, an inventor from Pittsburgh, developed a radio transmitter that could broadcast the human voice. Though it might seem mundane now, it was thought to be impossible at that time. On Christmas Eve, Fessenden tried his invention for the first time. That evening, wireless operators on ships, in newsrooms, and at railroad stations waiting for Morse code signals were shocked to hear a voice reading the second chapter of Luke. As he finished the scripture, Fessenden picked up his violin and played this French carol—the first song to be broadcast on wireless radio.

O holy night! The stars are brightly shining;
It is the night of the dear Savior's birth.
Long lay the world in sin and error pining,
Till He appeared and the soul felt its worth.
A thrill of hope—the weary world rejoices,
For yonder breaks a new and glorious morn!
Fall on your knees! O hear the angel voices!
O night divine, O night when Christ was born!
O night, O holy night, O night divine!

Led by the light of faith serenely beaming,
With glowing hearts by His cradle we stand.

So led by light of a star sweetly gleaming,
Here came the Wise Men from Orient land.
The King of kings lay thus in lowly manger,
In all our trials born to be our Friend.
He knows our need—to our weakness is no stranger.
Behold your King, before Him lowly bend!
Behold your King, before Him lowly bend!

Truly He taught us to love one another;
His law is love and His gospel is peace.
Chains shall He break, for the slave is our brother,
And in His name all oppression shall cease.
Sweet hymns of joy in grateful chorus raise we;
Let all within us praise His holy name.
Christ is the Lord! O praise His name forever!
His pow'r and glory evermore proclaim!
His pow'r and glory evermore proclaim!

Feed the One You Love!

With Santa on his way, why not leave him a few homemade whoopie pies? These cookies are everything your loved ones will want them to be and more. The cookies themselves are so moist and chewy, and the filling is just what a homemade whoopie pie filling should be—fluffy, sweet, and melt-in-your mouth delicious.

Red Velvet Whoopie Pies

Cookies

> 1½ cups all-purpose flour
>
> 2 Tbsp. unsweetened cocoa powder
>
> 1 tsp. baking soda
>
> ¼ tsp. baking powder
>
> ¼ tsp. salt
>
> 1 cup granulated sugar
>
> ½ cup unsalted butter, softened
>
> 1 large egg
>
> 1 Tbsp. liquid red food coloring

Filling

> 2 cups powdered sugar
>
> ½ cup vegetable shortening
>
> ½ cup unsalted butter, softened
>
> 1 Tbsp. hot water
>
> ½ tsp. vanilla extract

Position the oven racks in the upper and lower thirds of the oven, and preheat the oven to 375 degrees. Line a baking sheet with parchment paper or a silicone baking mat; set aside. In a mixing bowl whisk together flour, cocoa powder, baking soda, baking powder, and salt to combine. Using a stand mixer or hand mixer, cream together sugar and butter until pale and fluffy. Mix in egg and food coloring. With mixer set on low speed, add dry ingredients and mix until combined. Shape the dough into balls, about 1 tablespoon each, and place the dough balls 3-inches apart on the prepared baking sheets. Using your fingers, evenly flatten the dough balls slightly. Bake until the edges start setting, about 7-8 minutes. Cool on the baking sheet for a few minutes then transfer to a wire rack to cool completely.

To make the filling, use a stand mixer or hand mixer to beat together the powdered sugar, shortening, butter, water, and vanilla until light and fluffy. Place the filling in a pastry bag fitted with half-inch round tip (or carefully spoon mixture if you do not have a pastry bag). Turn half of the cookies over with bottoms facing upright and pipe about 1 tablespoon of the filling over cookies. Place remaining half of cookies over frosted cookies to sandwich cookies together.

Makes 12 sandwich cookies

December 25

Describing Jesus

"Allow the children to come to me," Jesus said. "Don't forbid them, because the kingdom of heaven belongs to people like these children."
MATTHEW 19:14

ALFRED BURT CREATED SOME OF THE WORLD'S most beautiful and moving Christmas carols in his thirty-three years of life. Before his death in 1953, he penned songs such as "Caroling, Caroling" and "The Star Carol." He also teamed with Wihla Hutson to compose "Some Children See Him." This song's lyrics examine the way children view Jesus. The song's verses point out that children from Africa likely see Him as black, while a Chinese child thinks of Jesus as having almond eyes. This carol has become an international favorite because it captures the universal nature of Jesus. He came for everyone. His chosen people are all people. So, naturally, when Christ enters the heart of a child, that child would see Him as being like him or her.

Jesus said that heaven belongs to people who are like children. What does this really mean? Over the last few weeks, we have talked about recapturing the enthusiasm and wonder we had as children. To look upon each moment as if it is new and something we have never before experienced.

Faith is much the same way. While we need to grown in knowledge, we don't need to become so adult we fail to hold onto childlike enthusiasm. In most cases it is a combination of Christian wisdom and joy that draws people to want to have the faith we possess. Children are born without prejudice and easily accept those who are different. Even very young children value character and compassion far more than they do appearance. Before they fall under worldly influence, children are very much like Christ. If we ridded ourselves of prejudice perhaps we would be too.

Consider this: nowhere in the Bible is there a description of Jesus. Even the renowned artists who created the most famous paintings of Christ had nothing to work from but their own imaginations. Therefore no one really knows what He looks like.

Maybe the Bible's writers didn't describe Christ because they couldn't. Possibly each of those who saw Jesus viewed Him as a child would. Perhaps Christ's appearance was as universal as His message. Maybe, because Jesus approached people without prejudice, everyone saw Him as their brother. So, if you were Mark, Luke, John, or Matthew, how could you describe someone everyone sees differently?

While not knowing what Jesus actually looks like might frustrate some, it also gives insight into what is really of value. For Christ words, actions, and character are of far more importance than appearance. Shouldn't this be the case in our world as well? Today is the day to get ready for our future home by becoming childlike in judgment.

Come Thou Long-Expected Jesus

After Isaac Watts, Charles Wesley might be the most revered early composer of hymns. In 1744, inspired by words he read in Haggai 2:7, the preacher sat down at a desk and penned "Come Thou Long-Expected Jesus." Wesley didn't consider this to be a Christmas song. In fact, he argued that his most powerful holiday anthem was "Love Divine All Loves Excelling," a hymn dealing with Christ's birth that was never adopted for Christmas use. "Come Thou Long-Expected Jesus" does reflect how long the world waited and how deeply it anticipated Christ's birth.

Come, thou long-expected Jesus,
born to set thy people free;
From our fears and sins release us,
let us find our rest in thee.
Israel's strength and consolation,
hope of all the earth thou art;
Dear desire of every nation,
joy of every longing heart.

Born thy people to deliver,
born a child and yet a King,
Born to reign in us forever,

now thy gracious kingdom bring.
By thine own eternal spirit
rule in all our hearts alone;
By thine all sufficient merit,
raise us to thy glorious throne.

Pamper the One You Love!

All mothers love to show off pictures of their kids and grandkids, and these personal photo coasters are a great way to do just that! By using just a few supplies from the local hardware store and your home, your loved one will be amazed after they see your creation.

Personal Photo Coasters

> 4 x 4-inch uncoated tiles (purchase extra for mistakes
> that might occur)
> colored printouts of your photos (use printer ink only
> and reverse the images)
> disposable gloves
> fingernail polish remover (with acetone)
> foam brush
> sheet of clear acetate
> metal spoon
> tile sealer
> sticky-back felt

Cut your images to fit the tiles. Heat the coaster in the microwave for a minute. (Heating the coaster helps the ink stick to the tile.) Place the image face down on the warm tile. Wearing gloves, pour some nail polish remover onto the foam brush and/or the color copy, coating the entire back of the image. Hold the image in place while applying the polish remover. Put the sheet of acetate over the back of the image and rub the entire surface with the back of a spoon (this will take some time to transfer). Remove the acetate and add more nail polish remover as it evaporates rather quickly. Occasionally stop and slowly lift the corners of the color copy to see if the ink is transferring. Don't worry if the paper sticks; it can be washed and rubbed off later. Once your image has transferred, you can remove the leftover paper from the color copy and wash it off with water. Apply a coat or two of tile sealer to the tile. Add sticky-back felt to the back. Wrap and give to those you love!

December 26

Boxing It Up

Then suppose that you were to take special notice of the one wearing
fine clothes, saying, "Here's an excellent place. Sit here." But to the
poor person you say, "Stand over there"; or, "Here, sit at my feet."
Wouldn't you have shown favoritism among yourselves and become
evil-minded judges? My dear brothers and sisters, listen! Hasn't
God chosen those who are poor by worldly standards to be rich in
terms of faith? Hasn't God chosen the poor as heirs of the kingdom
he has promised to those who love him?

JAMES 2:3-5

IN EVERY ENGLISH-SPEAKING COUNTRY except the United States, today is Boxing Day. The goals of Boxing Day actually reflect Christian
values even more than Christmas. To understand its importance you
have to go back to the 1200s. In the Middle Ages, churches throughout England kept small, antique metal boxes by the entry. Throughout the year, parishioners placed coins into those boxes. On December
26th, at the Feast of Saint Stephen, these "alms" boxes were opened,
and the money deposited there was distributed to the poorest of the
poor.

By 1500, the practice had expanded. Each servant brought an
empty box to homes where he or she worked and the employers placed

coins as well as the leftovers from the previous day's Christmas feast into those boxes. Within a century, those receiving gifts included bakers, blacksmiths, newspaper boys, butchers, and everyone else who provided services for the household. Today, Boxing Day is when people seek out the very poor and provide them with food, clothing, and money.

During Christ's day the Pharisees and others viewed poverty with disdain. In the thinking of that era, the poor deserved to be poor. In our time many have the same mind-set. Yet as Jesus proved during His ministry, and James wrote in scripture, the poor are not to be judged but to be helped. In Matthew, when Jesus urged His disciples to feed the poor, clothe the naked, care for the sick, and tend those in prison, He doesn't add a disclaimer that said, "Unless they have gotten themselves into this state because of sinful living, laziness, or poor judgment." He simply directed His followers to help those who needed it most.

A way to expand the spirit of Christmas for another twenty-four hours is to make Boxing Day your personal holiday. Rather than return items for refunds, find someone who could use those gifts. Today also might be a great time to create an alms box of your own. Place it near your entry, and each day drop your extra change into that container. You can even get your entire family involved as a way to teach them how to live out Christian compassion. Then on December 26th of next year, open that box and donate all that has been deposited to a person or organization in great need.

History tells us that one of the reasons the early church grew so rapidly was its members eagerly shared what they had with the poor without judgment. Perhaps it is time to emulate that kind of thinking and give in the spirit of Christ to those who are struggling right now. It is another profound way of living a sermon without saying a word.

I Gave My Life for Thee

Frances Ridley Havergal was the daughter of an Anglican priest and a poet. On a trip to Germany, a plaque under a painting of a crucified Jesus fascinated her. It read, "I gave my life for thee, what have you done for me?" Inspired, Havergal penned a poem, but after reading it was so unimpressed with her work she tossed it into the fire. When a puff of wind blew her poem away from the flames and onto the floor, she felt it was a sign God wanted her to keep it. Before she died in 1879, the verses she had tried to burn had become the framework for one of the greatest hymns in history.

I gave My life for thee;
My precious blood I shed,
That thou might ransomed be,
and quickened from the dead.
I gave, I gave My life for thee.
What hast thou giv'n for Me?
I gave, I gave My life for thee.
What hast thou giv'n for Me?

I spent long years for thee,
in weariness and woe,
That an eternity,
of joy thou mightest know.

I spent, I spent long years for thee.
Hast thou spent one for Me?
I spent, I spent long years for thee.
Hast thou spent one for Me?

My Father's house of light,
My glory-circled throne,
I left for earthly night,
for wand'rings sad and lone.
I left, I left it all for thee.
Hast thou left aught for Me?
I left, I left it all for thee.
Hast thou left aught for Me?

I suffered much for thee,
more than thy tongue can tell,
Of bitt'rest agony,
to rescue thee from hell.
I've borne, I've borne it all for thee.
What hast thou borne for Me?
I've borne, I've borne it all for thee.
What hast thou borne for Me?

And I have bro't to thee,
down from My home above,

Salvation full and free,

My pardon and My love.

I bring, I bring rich gifts to thee.

What hast thou brought to Me?

I bring, I bring rich gifts to thee.

What hast thou bro't to Me?

Feed the One You Love!

These yummy treats are perfect for little hands that need not to get dirty! They are also super easy to make and look like you worked on them for hours.

Dipped Cheesecake Pops

      1 16-oz. frozen cheesecake

      small ice cream scoop

      22-24 lollipop or wooden craft sticks

      1¾-2 cups white chocolate morsels

      1 Tbsp. vegetable oil or shortening

      ½ cup semisweet chocolate morsels

      colored sprinkles or sugars

Line a baking sheet with wax paper. Remove the cheesecake from the freezer; thaw for 5 minutes. Cut the cheesecake into 22-24 small even pieces. Press the cheesecake pieces, including crust, into the ice cream scoop. Working quickly, shape into 1½-inch balls. Press one lollipop stick into each cheesecake ball. Place on the prepared baking sheet and freeze for 1 hour. Microwave the white morsels and shortening in a dry, medium, uncovered, microwave-safe bowl on high for 45 seconds; stir. If needed, microwave at additional 15-second intervals, stirring vigorously after each interval until the morsels are melted. Dip the frozen cheesecake pops into the melted morsels, shake off the excess, and place them on the prepared baking sheet. Place the pops back in the freezer to allow chocolate to harden. Microwave the semi-sweet morsels in a small, uncovered, microwave-safe bowl on high power for 30 seconds; stir. If needed, microwave at additional 15-second intervals, stirring vigorously after each interval until the morsels are melted. Dip the bottom of the pops into the melted chocolate and decorate immediately with colored sprinkles or sugars. Freeze the pops until you are ready to serve. Allow them to soften for 5-10 minutes before serving.

Makes 22-24 pops

December 27

Standing Up for Others

The soldiers led Jesus away into the courtyard of the palace known as the governor's headquarters, and they called together the whole company of soldiers. They dressed him up in a purple robe and twisted together a crown of thorns and put it on him. They saluted him, "Hey! King of the Jews!" Again and again, they struck his head with a stick. They spit on him and knelt before him to honor him. When they finished mocking him, they stripped him of the purple robe and put his own clothes back on him. Then they led him out to crucify him. Simon, a man from Cyrene, Alexander and Rufus' father, was coming in from the countryside. They forced him to carry his cross.

MARK 15:16-21

IT CAN BE SO EASY TO LIVE A Christian life during the Christmas season. The babe in the manger is a symbol of joy and innocence. The nativity is nonthreatening, and the carols almost universally embrace a message of peace, hope, and love. But thirty years after Bethlehem, when this child grew into a man and challenged the establishment of His day, living as a Christian became difficult.

Through words and actions, the adult Jesus presented a radical new way of thinking. His message was not about war and conquest but about peace and acceptance. He was not nearly as concerned with following a rigid set of laws as He was in reaching out to those who had broken those ancient rules. In almost everything He did, He turned the religious establishment of that era upside down.

Today's scripture focuses on the journey from judgment to execution. Yet to fully put this text into focus we need to go back a full week. At that point Jesus was likely the most popular person on the planet. Thousands were lining the roads just to get a glimpse of Him. Everyone wanted to shake His hand or touch His robe. If there had been cameras then, people would have stood in long lines just to have a picture made with Christ. Can you imagine the pride His disciples must have felt? They likely told everyone who would listen, "Yes, I know Him well. In fact, I work with Jesus."

A week later the scene was far different. A few words here and a few lies there had turned the masses against the man they had recently fought to see. Their rage was so great they even intimidated the most powerful man in the city, Pilate, to release the innocent Jesus for execution. Surely there were those in that crowd who knew the truth, but they didn't speak up. Even the disciples remained hidden and mute as Christ walked those final miles.

Today oppressed and mistreated people are standing in for Christ. When the mob reacts to lies and turns on these innocents, will we be like those who stood by as Christ was crucified, or will we find the courage to stand up and speak up for Jesus? The choice is ours, and our faith will be defined by that choice.

Were You There

Perhaps no song in history asks a more haunting question. It is very easy to study the scene at the manger but much more difficult to fully visualize the crucifixion. To understand the gift given during that first Christmas, we must see a suffering Christ as clearly as we see the baby in the manger. The slave who wrote this song went to Calvary in his mind and soul, and what he witnessed obviously changed his view of the priceless gifts of faith, grace, and salvation.

Were you there when they crucified my Lord?
Were you there when they crucified my Lord?
Oh! sometimes it causes me to tremble, tremble,
    tremble.
Were you there when they crucified my Lord?

Were you there when they nailed him to the tree?
Were you there when they nailed him to the tree?
Oh! sometimes it causes me to tremble, tremble,
    tremble.
Were you there when they nailed him to the tree?

Were you there when they laid him in the tomb?
Were you there when they laid him in the tomb?

Oh! sometimes it causes me to tremble, tremble,
   tremble.
Were you there when they laid him in the tomb?

Were you there when God raised him from the tomb?
Were you there when God raised him from the tomb?
Oh! sometimes it causes me to tremble, tremble,
   tremble.
Were you there when God raised him from the tomb?

Pamper the One You Love!

If you have never made candles before, these beeswax candles are a great place to begin. They are easy to make and can be personalized for any special occasion. Our simple and easy-to-follow instructions will make wonderful gifts for the ones you love!

Lemon Beeswax Candles

> 2 12-oz. jars
> 1 pound of beeswax (pellets)
> slow cooker
> lemon essential oil (1 Tbsp. per container)
> candle wicks

Fill the jars with 8 oz. each of beeswax pellets. Place them in the slow cooker with just enough water to partially submerge the containers. Leave on a low heat for a few minutes while the wax melts. Once the wax is melted, stir in the lemon essential oil (use disposable utensils or equipment specifically reserved for candle making). Carefully remove the jars from the slow cooker. As the candle begins to harden, push the wick to the bottom of the jar. The wax will harden the wick in place. Allow the candle to cool for at least 4 hours or overnight.

December 28

Extending the Spirit of Christmas

The law of the Spirit of life in Christ Jesus has set you free from the law of sin and death.

ROMANS 8:2

THREE DAYS AGO IT WAS THE MOST wonderful time of the year; now it seems the joy and spirit that marked Christ's birth are being packed away like the lights and decorations. As trees make their way out of living rooms to curbs and Christmas carols are replaced by secular tunes, it is little wonder so many are depressed. What seems so long coming has so quickly gone away. As we are hit with the winter blues, we wonder why every day can't be like Christmas.

On a hot summer night in 1965, Memphis songwriter Red West was invited to the Memphian Theater. Elvis Presley had rented the movie house for an all-night film marathon. Not long after arriving, West was enveloped in a holidaylike spirit. There was laughter everywhere, and the king of rock-and-roll had brought presents for everyone. West noted to a friend that it felt just like Christmas.

After returning home, West picked up a newspaper. The news was

bleak. American soldiers were dying in Vietnam, students were protesting that war, and race riots had broken out in the nation's largest cites. Contrasting the spirit of the party he had just left to the state of the world, the songwriter picked up pen and paper. It took West just three hours to write a song highlighting how different the world would be if every day was like Christmas. Elvis told friends that West's modern carol was his favorite holiday song. Others must have felt the same way because "If Every Day Was Like Christmas" quickly became a seasonal classic. In his inspired lyrics, the songwriter painted a vivid picture of why December 25th was so special, however he didn't offer a recipe to take that feeling over to the rest of the year.

The fact is, the world doesn't change at Christmas, people do. It is the attitude of individuals that makes Christmas seem so special. So though the holiday songs and decorations might be gone for the next eleven months, there is no law that says we have to pack away the Christmas spirit. After all, the Truth we celebrated on December 25th is still the Truth. The Christ who was born in a manger and nailed to a cross is still alive and with us. So, with that in mind, why shouldn't we still feel the same wonder, excitement, and grace on December 28th or July 14th as we do on December 25th?

If we choose, we can be just as happy, welcoming, and giving today as we were three days ago. To do so we must embrace the spirit of Christmas and let it shine in our eyes and define our actions. After all, *Christmas* means worship Christ. With that truth in mind, every day that we continue to worship our Lord should be just like Christmas.

The Wassail Song

Wassailing was an English tradition born out of necessity. In the winter many poor families did not have enough food. Their survival often depended upon the generosity of others. Children were sent out with bowls to sing at the homes of the wealthy in hopes their songs would generate a bit of goodwill, a scrap of food, or a copper coin. The wassail bowl was often the only thing standing between poor children and death from starvation.

Here we come a wassailing
among the leaves so green,
Here we come a wandering
so fair to be seen.
Love and joy come to you,
and to you your wassail too,
And God bless you and send you a happy New Year
and God send you a happy New Year.

Our wassail cup is made
of the rosemary tree,
And so is your beer
of the best barley.
Love and joy come to you,

and to you your wassail too,
And God bless you and send you a happy New Year
and God send you a happy New Year.

We are not daily beggars
that beg from door to door,
But we are neighbours' children
whom you have seen before.
Love and joy come to you,
and to you your wassail too,
And God bless you and send you a happy New Year
and God send you a happy New Year.

We have a little purse
made of ratching leather skin;
We want some of your small change
to line it well within.
Love and joy come to you,
and to you your wassail too,
And God bless you and send you a happy New Year
and God send you a happy New Year.

Call up the Butler of this house,
put on his golden ring;
Let him bring us up a glass of beer,

and the better we shall sing.
Love and joy come to you,
and to you your wassail too,
And God bless you and send you a happy New Year
and God send you a happy New Year.

Bring us out a table,
and spread it with a cloth;
Bring us out a mouldy cheese,
and some of your Christmas loaf.
Love and joy come to you,
and to you your wassail too,
And God bless you and send you a happy New Year
and God send you a happy New Year.

God bless the Master of this house,
Likewise the Mistress too;
And all the little children
that round the table go.
Love and joy come to you,
and to you your wassail too,
And God bless you and send you a happy New Year
and God send you a happy New Year.

Feed the One You Love!

What little child doesn't love sugar cookies with sprinkles on top? Well, how about putting sprinkles in the middle! This easy recipe gives the cookies a cake batter–like taste, and they are loaded with sprinkles! The recipe is fast, easy to make, and won't disappoint!

Sprinkle Sugar Cookies

½ cup (1 stick) unsalted butter, softened

¾ cup granulated sugar

1 large egg

1½ tsp. clear vanilla extract

1½ tsp. almond extract

1½ cups all-purpose flour

2 tsp. corn starch

¾ tsp. baking soda

pinch salt, optional and to taste

¾ cup sprinkles

Using a pastry blender or heavy-duty stand mixer with paddle attached on low speed, combine the butter, sugar, egg, and extracts and beat on medium-high speed until well-creamed, light, and fluffy, about 5 minutes (or use a hand mixer and beat for at least 7 minutes). Do not shortcut the creaming process; make sure dough is very light in color and fluffy, stopping to scrape down the sides of the mixer as necessary. When the mixture creams, scrape down the sides of the bowl and add the flour, cornstarch, baking soda, and optional salt. Mix until just combined, about 1 minute. Add the sprinkles and beat momentarily to incorporate, less than 1 minute, or fold in by hand. Using a 2-inch cookie scoop or spoon, form heaping 2-tablespoon mounds. Place mounds on a large plate, flatten mounds slightly with your palm, cover with plastic wrap, and refrigerate for at least 2 hours or up to 5 days before baking. Preheat oven to 350 degrees. Line a baking sheet with parchment paper or a silicone baking mat. Place mounds on baking sheets, spaced at least 2 inches apart. Bake for 8 minutes, or until edges have set and tops are just beginning to set, even if undercooked, pale, and glossy in the center. These cookies should not turn golden or brown at all; they should stay white. Do not overbake; cookies will firm up as they cool. Allow cookies to cool on the baking sheet for about 5 minutes before removing and transferring to a rack to finish cooling.

Makes 15 medium cookies

December 29

A Symbol of the Power of Faith

If I speak in tongues of human beings and of angels but I don't have love, I'm a clanging gong or a clashing cymbal. If I have the gift of prophecy and I know all the mysteries and everything else, and if I have such complete faith that I can move mountains but I don't have love, I'm nothing....Love is patient, love is kind, it isn't jealous, it doesn't brag, it isn't arrogant, it isn't rude, it doesn't seek its own advantage, it isn't irritable, it doesn't keep a record of complaints, it isn't happy with injustice, but it is happy with the truth. Love puts up with all things, trusts in all things, hopes for all things, endures all things.

Love never fails. As for prophecies, they will be brought to an end. As for tongues, they will stop. As for knowledge, it will be brought to an end. We know in part and we prophesy in part; but when the perfect comes, what is partial will be brought to an end. When I was a child, I used to speak like a child, reason like a child, think like a child. But now that I have become a man, I've put an end to childish things. Now we see a reflection in a mirror; then we will see face-to-face. Now I know partially, but then I will know completely in the same way that I have been completely known. Now faith, hope, and love remain—these three things—and the greatest of these is love.

1 CORINTHIANS 13:1-13

ONE OF THE CHRISTMAS SEASON'S MOST unusual symbols is mistletoe. Though initially wrapped in folklore and superstition, thanks to early missionaries, mistletoe is also ripe with Christian meaning. In fact, long before most people could read, the mistletoe plant was employed as a way of explaining Christ's life, sacrifice, and gift of salvation.

Scandinavian warriors believed mistletoe was the most powerful plant in the forest. At that time this evergreen shoot stood for the eternal life and the power of the gods. There was even a law that if warring tribes met in areas where mistletoe grew, they had to cease fighting. Therefore mistletoe became a symbol of peace. Early missionaries explained that the living mistletoe plant growing out of a seemingly dead tree represented the Prince of Peace who had been nailed to the wooden cross. The plant's white berries embodied His innocence and the red berries His shed blood. The green leaves were the promise of grace and eternal life for those who believed in and served this Lord.

Early Christians put such great stock in this symbolism that they posted mistletoe plants over their doors to proclaim their faith. When a man and woman were married, mistletoe was even hung over the altar. During the ceremony the couple was reminded that as long as they kept God at the center of their lives, like mistletoe, they would survive even the darkest and most trying times. Naturally, after the wedding vows, the newlywed's first act was to kiss under the mistletoe.

Today the only element of the plant's history that has survived concerns kissing. But the Bible teaches us what has been lost can be found and restored. So mistletoe can still serve as a reminder that if we embrace deep faith we can survive the greatest tests of life; and by sharing a brief history of mistletoe with others, we can also open the door to explaining our Christian faith in simple but profound terms. So maybe we should just leave the mistletoe over our doors all year long.

Stand Up, Stand Up for Jesus

In the days before the American Civil War, Dudley A. Tyng was one of the nation's most revered evangelists. After a successful crusade, Tyng visited a farm and was somehow caught in a mechanical corn sheller. His injuries were so severe that the attending doctor could do nothing to save him. Just before he died, the preacher looked up to his friends and family and said, "Stand up for Jesus." George Duffield worked those last words into a song and sang "Stand Up, Stand Up for Jesus" for the first time at Tyng's funeral.

Stand up, stand up for Jesus,
ye soldiers of the cross;
Lift high his royal banner,
it must not suffer loss.
From victory unto victory
his army shall he lead,
Till every foe is vanquished,
and Christ is Lord indeed.

Stand up, stand up for Jesus,
the trumpet call obey;
Forth to the mighty conflict,
in this his glorious day.

Ye that are brave now serve him
against unnumbered foes;
Let courage rise with danger,
and strength to strength oppose.

Stand up, stand up for Jesus,
stand in his strength alone;
The arm of flesh will fail you,
ye dare not trust your own.
Put on the gospel armor,
each piece put on with prayer;
Where duty calls or danger,
be never wanting there.

Stand up, stand up for Jesus,
the strife will not be long;
This day the noise of battle,
the next the victor's song.
To those who vanquish evil
a crown of life shall be;
they with the King of Glory
shall reign eternally.

Pamper the One You Love!

Don't have time to go to the spa or get a pedicure? How about just taking some time for yourself and enjoying a stress-relieving foot soak? These ingredients will soften your skin, remove toxins, add magnesium to your body, and thanks to the essential oils, relax you! It's just like being at the spa, but minus the price tag.

Homemade (Stress-Relieving) Foot Soak

> 1 cup sea salt
> 1 cup Epsom salt
> 2 cups baking soda
> 12-15 drops of your favorite essential oil(s)
> sealable jar

Combine sea salt, Epsom salt, and baking soda in a large bowl; mix well. Add the drops of your favorite essential oil or combination of oils. Using a spoon, mix the ingredients again to distribute the oil(s) throughout the mixture. Once combined, store in a sealable jar. When you are ready to use it, pour about ¼ cup of the salt/oil mixture into a bowl or pan large enough for your feet. Add hot water (as hot as you can stand) then add feet! Grab a good book or a fun magazine and soak for 15 minutes or up to 1 hour.

For foot soaks or baths, try the following essentials oils:

Eucalyptus is a powerful antibacterial, antiviral soak.

Lavender is great for a relaxing soak.

Lime is a good choice for a refreshing and invigorating soak.

Peppermint is used for a refreshing, cooling, and soothing soak. Peppermint also has anti-inflammatory properties.

Tea Tree can be used as a disinfectant or antifungal for things like athlete's foot.

December 30

This Little Light

"You are the light of the world. A city on top of a hill can't be hidden. Neither do people light a lamp and put it under a basket. Instead, they put it on top of a lampstand, and it shines on all who are in the house. In the same way, let your light shine before people, so they can see the good things you do and praise your Father who is in heaven."

MATTHEW 5:14-16

BETWEEN THANKSGIVING AND New Year's, the world is filled with light. The tradition of Christmas lights began about five hundred years ago when Martin Luther was walking through a forest on a cold winter's night and noted the starlight filtering through pines. Inspired, he raced home, found a candle, and tied it to the family's Christmas tree. As he lit that candle, he explained to his children that the flame represented the light that came into a dark world when Christ was born.

From Luther's idea of using a candle as a teaching tool, the concept of Christmas lights has grown to where hundreds of billions of bulbs of varying colors are used during each holiday season. They decorate trees, homes, yards, buildings, and even storefronts all over the world. I must admit that my wife and I do our part. We decorate to the

max! We have as many as six full-size Christmas trees and a yard filled with lights and decorations. The entire process of making our holidays bright takes more than a week of work.

Last year, as I was beginning to take down all those lights, a neighbor asked, "Why do you go to all that trouble and expense?" I explained the lights are not for us; we do it so others can enjoy them. And we receive scores of thank-you notes each year proving they do. It is all about lifting spirits.

Christmas lights usually stay up for about five weeks. That leaves forty-seven more weeks when the world does not shine nearly as bright. During those times it becomes our responsibility to be the light. It is what we are called to do. We are not to shine just on Christmas Day; we are to reflect the light that came into the world in that Bethlehem stable each day we live. And if we believe that Jesus is the Son of God, we shouldn't need to plug in our soul's light for it to shine. That light should be seen in our actions toward others. It should be read in the way we live out Christ's teachings. It should shine brightly when we greet others with both welcoming smiles and kind words, and it shines brightest when we love freely without prejudice and leave the judging to God.

As you take down your holiday lights, make a resolution to shine as if it is Christmas each day of the new year. If you do, your light will lead others to brighter places, a more hopeful world, and a happier life. Let your light shine!

Amazing Grace

The story behind "Amazing Grace" is well-known. John Newton penned the lyrics to share his personal journey from sinner to salvation. Later, Newton, a one-time slave ship sailor, would use the song to lead the fight against the institution that he had once supported. The popularity of this hymn fully reflects what Jesus's birth meant, and still means, to the world. Jesus was not just a baby born on the first Christmas; God's grace was delivered by that birth, and that changed everything.

Amazing Grace! How sweet the sound
that saved a wretch like me!
I once was lost, but now am found;
was blind, but now I see.

'Twas grace that taught my heart to fear,
and grace my fears relieved;
How precious did that grace appear
the hour I first believed.

Through many dangers, toils, and snares,
I have already come;
'Tis grace hath brought me safe thus far,
And grace will lead me home.

The Lord has promised good to me,
his word my hope secures;
He will my shield and portions be,
as long as life endures.

Feed the One You Love!

There is something delightfully refreshing about citrus fruits, and especially the lemon. Give these tasty cookies as a gift, or serve them at a party—they taste delicious and take only a few minutes to make!

Easy Lemon Crackle Cookies

    lemon cake mix
    2 eggs
    ⅓ cup vegetable oil
    zest of 1 lemon
    juice of 1 lemon
    ⅓ cup powdered sugar

Preheat the oven to 375 degrees. Line a baking sheet with parchment paper or a silicone baking mat; set aside. Mix the cake mix, eggs, oil, lemon zest, and lemon juice in a large bowl. Refrigerate the dough for at least 30 minutes. Roll tablespoon-sized balls of dough in the powdered sugar. Coat them well and place them on the baking sheet. Bake for 9 minutes. Allow the cookies to cool on the baking sheet for about 5 minutes before transferring them to a rack to finish cooling.

Makes 24 cookies

December 31

Living a Calling

We have many parts in one body, but the parts don't all have the same function. In the same way, though there are many of us, we are one body in Christ, and individually we belong to each other. We have different gifts that are consistent with God's grace that has been given to us.

ROMANS 12:4-6

"AULD LANG SYNE" IS ONE OF THE MOST familiar songs on earth. Yet this traditional New Year's anthem was not considered a holiday classic until December 31, 1929. At midnight on that night, Guy Lombardo and His Royal Canadians played the song on a national radio broadcast from the Waldorf Astoria Hotel. Suddenly millions of Americans had the mistaken impression that the legendary English poet Robert Burns had penned "Auld Lang Syne" just to welcome in the New Year.

Tonight, all over the world, that old song will be sung once again. Also tonight millions will embrace another tradition—writing resolutions. Of course the great joke about resolutions is they are always made but never kept. So perhaps this year we don't need to pen resolutions but rather resolve to find and use a calling.

Callings can come in all areas of life. God calls people as preachers and missionaries, and also teachers, nurses, lawyers, doctors, farmers, and so many other things. There is no better example of God using a person outside the realm of normal Christian callings than Branch Rickey.

As a teen, Rickey felt he was called to be a baseball player, but his parents and church did not agree. They felt God could only use the young man as a preacher. After much prayer Rickey tried his hand at professional baseball. When he failed, people in his family and church said, "I told you so." Yet he refused to give up on his calling. After gaining a law degree, Rickey worked his way into baseball management but for thirty years found little success. Finally, well into his fifties, he shaped the 1930s St. Louis Cardinals into a winner. Suddenly recognized as a genius and considered one of the most powerful figures in sports, he took over as general manager of the Brooklyn Dodgers. In 1946, in the face of public wrath, he called upon his Christian faith to right a wrong. When Rickey integrated baseball, he helped kick-start the civil rights movement. Soon thereafter he used his growing wealth to become one of the first investors in *Guideposts Magazine*. A few years later he helped found the Fellowship of Christian Athletes. Thus, in a very secular position, he was able to boldly live out his calling though both words and actions and change both life and faith for millions.

Like Branch Rickey, God has a calling for you. Even if you never preach a sermon or go on the mission field, He has a spiritual purpose for your life. This is the moment to examine where and how He

wants you to serve. You might be in that place already and have just failed to realize it was your calling, or you might have ignored that calling because you couldn't see how your faith could be used in that position. This is the time to pray and follow God's lead into the New Year. This is the moment to begin searching for your calling! This is the day to resolve to embrace your special gift.

Auld Lang Syne

In 1788, Robert Burns quoted a Scottish song while writing a letter to his friend and critic Frances Anna Dunlap. In that correspondence Burns also shared new verses inspired by the old folk standard. After the poet set those words to a familiar tune, "Auld Lang Syne" became one of England's most popular pub songs. Ultimately the lyrics reflected Burns's unique and rocky friendship with Dunlap and how much he valued her honestly and loyalty. On his deathbed, the last words Burns read was from a letter written by his treasured pen pal.

Should auld acquaintance be forgot,
and never bro't to mind?
Should auld acquaintance be forgot,
and auld lang syne?
For auld lang syne, my dear,
for auld lang syne,
We'll take a cup of kindness yet,
for auld lang syne.

And surely you'll buy your pint cup!
and surely I'll buy mine!
And we'll take a cup o' kindness yet,

for auld lang syne.
For auld lang syne, my dear,
for auld lang syne,
We'll take a cup of kindness yet,
for auld lang syne.

We two have run about the slopes,
and picked the daisies fine;
But we've wandered many a weary foot,
since auld lang syne.
For auld lang syne, my dear,
for auld lang syne,
We'll take a cup of kindness yet,
for auld lang syne.

We two have paddled in the stream,
from morning sun till dine[†];
But seas between us broad have roared
since auld lang syne.
For auld lang syne, my dear,
for auld lang syne,
We'll take a cup of kindness yet,
for auld lang syne.

And there's a hand my trusty friend!
And give me a hand o' thine!

And we'll take a right good-will draught,
for auld lang syne.
For auld lang syne, my dear,
for auld lang syne,
We'll take a cup of kindness yet,
for auld lang syne.

Pamper the One You Love!

Homemade Peppermint Sugar Scrub makes the perfect handmade gift. It exfoliates, moisturizes, and leaves your skin feeling super soft and smelling amazing!

Peppermint Sugar Scrub in a Jar

> 2 cups sugar
>
> ¼ cup coconut oil
>
> peppermint essential oil or peppermint extract
>
> red food coloring
>
> 1 pint-sized glass jar

Pour sugar into a medium-sized bowl. Mix in the coconut oil (add more if you like a moist consistency). Add a few drops of the peppermint essential oil. Divide the sugar mixture into two portions of equal size. Mix in a few drops of red food coloring to one portion (making it pink). Pour the mixture into the jar in layers (alternating the pink and white). Apply pressure to the sugar scrub using a small spoon to make it more compact. Wrap with a red and white ribbon and decorative tag.